LIFE - Let It Flow Effortlessly

LET IT FLOW
EFFORTLESSLY

HOW BEING GENUINE CREATES REAL VALUE

NORMA STRANGE

NEW YORK

LONDON • NASHVILLE • MELBOURNE • VANCOUVER

LIFE - LET IT FLOW EFFORTLESSLY

HOW BEING GENUINE CREATES REAL VALUE

© 2019 Norma Strange

Published in New York, New York, by Morgan James Publishing. Morgan James is a trademark of Morgan James, LLC. www.MorganJamesPublishing.com

The Morgan James Speakers Group can bring authors to your live event. For more information or to book an event visit The Morgan James Speakers Group at www.TheMorganJamesSpeakersGroup.com.

ISBN 9781683508892 paperback
ISBN 9781683508908 eBook
Library of Congress Control Number: 2017918835

Cover Design by:
Chris Treccani
www.3dogcreative.net

Interior Design by:
Christopher Kirk
www.GFSstudio.com

In an effort to support local communities, raise awareness and funds, Morgan James Publishing donates a percentage of all book sales for the life of each book to Habitat for Humanity Peninsula and Greater Williamsburg.

Get involved today! Visit
www.MorganJamesBuilds.com

DEDICATION

" **M**om… you have your life and I have my life!" Casey, my oldest daughter, summed this up so simply at the early age of 3 years old. More than simple, it was pure and has never stopped echoing throughout my life. My life has been enriched because now, I truly own it. It's mine. And yours is yours. You can waste time living yours for someone else, but why? There's an unmatched freedom that comes from understanding and really accepting this idea.

If you don't consider yourself capable, worthy or able, this book was written for you—to realize your own worth. Remember, you are priceless. Each of us has our own understanding of our existence. I hope you won't let anyone convince you to give up on you, especially yourself.

This book is dedicated to the many people like my daughter who've inspired me and taught me valuable lessons. The people who just wouldn't shrink to limiting labels the world tried to pin on them. The people who became bigger than their limits. Some battled health, financial or life challenges that seemed too big to overcome. And yet, they didn't quit. Somehow each found a way to claim their power back from the situation that threatened it, and continued to press on and live fully.

My hope is that you utilize this life letting it flow effortlessly to be genuine and create real value. It always confused me that so much energy is focused on making a living, when we were given life freely. It seems common to get caught up into spending time and precious life to exchange for money to fund a lifestyle as we seek value. I wrote this to help us flip this around. You are value. You matter. You are priceless. You are unlimited. Your story matters. Inspiration breeds an inner strength that is contagious and it starts with you. This book is dedicated to you. I hope it brings out your very best. We have the potential to change the world together as you embrace fulfillment and see what happens when you overflow onto others.

TABLE OF CONTENTS

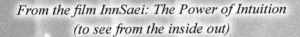

From the film InnSaei: The Power of Intuition
(to see from the inside out)

"To see within is to know yourself.
To know yourself well enough
to be able to put yourself into other people's shoes
and to bring out the best in you."

FOREWORD

Every so often, you are introduced to something that appears to be explicitly simple and basic yet immensely profound. I experienced that very feeling as I read the manuscript for this book. First of all, the size of this book appealed to me because I knew it could be a quick read. However, I soon realized that I was engaged in what felt to be a conversation with the author, Norma Strange.

LIFE – Let It Flow Effortlessly: How Being Genuine Creates Real Value is a wonderful collection of experiences and the thoughts, philosophies and principles that formed from them to become a simple process for fulfillment and success. This work is important for anyone to engage. It's applicable to anyone desiring to improve their results—not just business owners, leaders and working professionals. Personal development is the foundation to designing your life for success.

My near 50 years of experience, directly and indirectly, in first building a successful direct selling business and later leading and coaching others has unequivocally convinced me; Success is about becoming the person you can be, and then about helping others become what they can be!

Norma carefully shows you, step by step, how to be all you can be! And what happens to the world and those around as you experience so much fulfillment, you overflow into their lives. This book is an excellent read for anyone who hasn't really realized... Your success will not be contingent upon the products or services you sell or represent. It's all about the real value, the genuine YOU can make.

John Fleming
Former Publisher/Editor in Chief of Direct Selling News,
DSN Ambassador

PREFACE

How one person can positively impact another's and the way this changes our collective life experience captured my imagination and created the spark to write this book. Together, the difference you and I make is to give a human spirit the power to be fulfilled; that's how we shine. I realized that simple things I did naturally or beliefs that I adopted were the seeds to producing great results.

Reading this book not only impacts you and your results. As we strengthen individuals and lead organizations to be more effective, we support families, create jobs, build businesses and accelerate opportunities while we strengthen our nation and the world to have economic strength. Improving your own understanding first of yourself and then of those around you will empower you to connect more quickly and much deeper. This is important as collaboration is becoming more important to business success. Brands create communities.

It's no secret that a team is much stronger and capable of accomplishing more than one individual alone. No one gets to the top alone. There are all kinds of inputs that contribute to success. Seek to build success for yourself but not by yourself. As you have a clear vision, share your passion with those relationships around you, and you'll attract people who resonate with your vision who want to help. It works so much better and faster when you work with people to build everyone's success together.

This book engages the power of your heart and the potential of your mind to guide you to achieve fulfillment. I'm here speaking to you in this book to help you discover what's already inside you that will let you enjoy life. When it's flowing effortlessly you can reach your goals being genuine, making a difference in the most real and meaningful way possible. As you take action, value is given. Making money or feeling a sense of accomplishment—that is simply value received. This is the reciprocity of value. If you are willing, this book will prepare you for more accomplishment more effortlessly than you ever imagined possible. Let it flow and it will be fun! No one sets limits on us. It is merely our perspective and lack of creativity that blinds us from seeing our potential.

Success is seen as attitude revealed through your presence. Your presence alone has value, but your success isn't just about you or the product or service you represent. When you know and value you, it becomes more natural to listen to people on a deeper level. It feels effortless being this genuine. You deliver more value and serve the real needs of people. Operating in this way gives you a distinct advantage. Your reward is not just more customers but creating life-long advocates who champion your success. It's better than any marketing system continuing to perform no matter the economic environment. What better position is there than to have a mass of people generously opening doors, making introductions, or even marketing your product or service for you? This is the power of edification and endorsement. It's a valuable asset to you, your profession, and your business. It's fully in your control to design this outcome to relate and connect rather than just market or sell. People love to buy and they buy what they value.

For those readers who are in the direct selling industry, imagine empowering more people to achieve success with less frustration. Since success in direct selling or network marketing is reflective of becoming an effective leader and duplicating your leadership into a volunteer team, it is imperative to strengthen yourself first and then learn how to build strong relationships and inspire other people to follow your lead to create a strong team. Any team in business, government, non-profit, or local community could benefit from learning and applying these principles. Our success is realized in building strong communities.

As I've worked face to face with professionals, entrepreneurs, business owners and team leaders, I've discovered the importance of sharing simple proven principles and education that really works. From teaching the content of this book in consultations and workshops, I've witnessed dramatic breakthroughs, life changes, and accelerated results. Of course, it's ultimately up to each individual to choose to stay with their development until they reach their goal. Remember, no one can do the work for another. All we can do is to lead and instruct people to follow a recipe. Ultimately, we each choose to receive success when we are ready.

For those who are currently employed, don't check out on me just yet. You still have the ability to create a positive impact even if you are working for someone else. I found early in my career that even as I was employed by someone else, my success was dependent on having a business-owner mindset. I played the game of work to run my job as if I was the business owner of my employee chair. I took responsibility for the things within my job boundaries. As I understood the rules of the game of being an employee, I would excel in the areas I could affect. I even took on projects outside my job responsibilities increasing my value to the company. Adopting a business-owner mindset catapulted me to achieve higher pay and more promotions than any other single piece of advice I could share with you.

I've often wondered why people work so hard to make a living when they've been given LIFE. This thought pattern will set the stage for your transformation. Think about what your life would look like if you embraced all of your time knowing you could do anything with this vital resource. Imagine that all of your bills are paid and that you have enough money for anything needed, and even some to spare! Imagine you have all of your time, and you have money providing for your livelihood. Now, instead of having to go *do* something for work, what would you *be*? If you didn't make limits appear real, who would you let yourself be if you lived unlimited, living LIFE effortlessly?

I'm excited for you.

HOW ARE
YOU?

HOW ARE YOU?

So, really—how are you?

No matter the current situation or economic circumstance, you can be successful if you're willing to check in with yourself first. As Henry Ford states, "Whether you believe you can or can't, you are right!" Who chooses your success? You do! That is why it is so important to begin the work of strengthening your mindset by identifying and removing your limiting beliefs. If you're unaware of these limits, you may not realize the sabotage they can create just as you feel you're gaining successful momentum. It's best to do some work to identify what's holding you back. That's why you're here.

People who've met me comment that they think I am magical, psychic or some sort of angel. This sounds pretty funny and is definitely weird, but it's because of how foreign to them it is to have someone, some strange person, give so much attention to them or have someone seem so genuinely interested in their success.

I wasn't always able to be so free with my compassion and care. I'm sure I just came like this, but I lost the willingness to be vulnerable just like many do. And it didn't take long for me to learn that sometimes others weren't about my best interests. Between growing up with siblings and surrendering to the education system it's easy to lose yourself. Having parents who haven't done personal development work and aren't any closer to self-actualizing themselves, will have you running from genuine connectedness and collaboration. You may develop a strong belief that unconditional love won't survive in our world.

I'm here to share that it can be found. You are in there and you're perfect just the way you are. Your genuine self has immense value. How does that feel? You may disagree with me, but that's okay. There's something here in this human experiment that is uniquely yours. And it can be extraordinary if you let it. So how are you right now? If you're open to exploring the inner depths of your existence, you could decide once and for all to really be you and see the great results.

I am here to encourage you through The LIFE Process. It's simple but very powerful. It's not something you do. It's who you become in the process that's the result. It's transformational.

This book is designed to facilitate your development. It's written as if we are having a conversation. It's not intended to give you answers but to get you thinking. This requires your participation. The goal is not to consume this as fast as possible; it's to apply this work to your life right now. You have the power to create your life to a desired outcome just as any artist creates a masterpiece.

I'm here to help you claim your power and embrace the powerful success you were created to be. I see my role here as a mentor. We'll walk together through these pages just as I have done in many live seminars as I taught this material to others who wanted results. I'm here to guide you, question you and cause you to reflect your steps to gain clarity.

If you want to read through this book to gain an overview or consume everything quickly, take a moment to consider what you'll miss. Understand that our life's work is not about getting to the finish line. It's about the journey. Don't miss out on the value you can gain by re-reading and spending time to apply this material to your life. I find that as you live this rather than skim through it, additional insights are uncovered as you formulate a deeper relationship with what you are learning.

It is a fact that if you just read through this book, you'll only retain about 10% it. Responding to the journal questions will increase your comprehension and deepen your understanding and development. As you answer the questions, journaling will clarify your LIFE Process and you'll naturally think about these concepts as you live your life. Add to the questions and share your experiences with us and our online community. Feel free to blog about The LIFE Process and teach it to others. The best way to learn is to experience the whole process – discovery, development, and passing on your insight and the wisdom you've gained. Imagine what a difference you'll make as you let your LIFE flow effortlessly and create real value everywhere! Imagine leaders who've refined their development overseeing communities across the world. Can you see the ripple effect this can have? And everywhere people embracing their own uniqueness and contributing generously while knowing they are valuable, priceless and brilliant!

I've found that people can do unlimited things if they believe they can. It's as if they had so much conviction, there was no possibility of failure. Do you believe in you? We'll get there. I promise—if you're willing.

Here are some of the foundational beliefs I've benefitted from for you to consider adopting and living by:

- ❏ I am priceless and my life has purpose.
- ❏ I can help others celebrate their wins without diminishing any of my own possibility.
- ❏ I live in abundance.
- ❏ Adopting a business-owner mindset will help me be the best at my work.
- ❏ I am in business for myself, not by myself.
- ❏ Relationships help me reach my potential.
- ❏ My fulfillment is accelerated by the positive choices I make.
- ❏ People everywhere will help my inspired vision.
- ❏ My results reflect my current level of knowledge and effectiveness. Both can be improved.
- ❏ My experiences matter. They make me stronger and wiser.
- ❏ There will be setbacks and only I can quit on my success. Failure is an attitude.
- ❏ I can reach my goals faster than I've ever imagined.
- ❏ There is enough time for everything I want to do.
- ❏ I am responsible and accountable for my own life.
- ❏ I always have a choice. I can succeed.

Do these statements sound foreign or even make you feel uncomfortable? Which one of these jumps out at you? Read them again, out loud—slowly—and pay attention to how your body reacts as you say them. Just begin noticing more of how your body communicates with you. This will help you exercise your inner guide to help on your journey to fulfillment.

Here's where we start. I believe in you. See those words. I believe in you. Reread it if you need to but seriously, I believe in you. Now, say it in your head, "I believe in you."

As you take steps toward letting life flow effortlessly, keep in mind—this is simple. You were created to be you and none other. You have unique talents, thoughts, insights… so many that you have bottled up for however many years you are old. Allow yourself to play. We are just going to play and allow you to be safe to discover what you've always dreamed of—LIFE without limits by being genuinely you.

I care about you and want you to be aware of how you are now and as you do this inner transformative work. The more you can be honest with yourself, the faster you will progress. But don't rush it. You are not competing with anyone but yourself.

It's like you've fallen into a mud puddle. I see you there all muddy and embarrassed. Instead of pointing fingers and gathering my friends to laugh at you and revel in our superior situation, I am sitting down in the mud puddle with you. We both know it's uncomfortable, but we're sitting here nonetheless. I used to offer to pull people out of the mud, but I've found that hurts my back and some resist trying to pull me in the puddle with them. So we sit here covered in cold yucky mud. How are you? How do you feel? What do you want? What will you do? What's possible now?

Nothing happens for you in this mud puddle. You see, I decided to be in the puddle with you but you think it is an accident you're in the puddle. It just happened to you. You hate the puddle, the embarrassment, the cold slippery feeling of the mud. This is your current life. Ah, but once we would have imagined our entire day away playing in the puddle. That's how you know you've lost it too.

There's so much we can do… so much *you* can do. This is an invitation. It's no coincidence that we are having this talk.

You're ready aren't you? Let's stand up and see where our first steps lead us.

To get the greatest value out of our time together, I invite you to commit to writing in a notebook or journal to answer the questions I ask as we go along. Think of me as your mentor and the pace is yours to set. The questions aren't designed to be rhetorical or answered and just left. Capture thoughts and feelings you experience as you consider your sincere answers. All of them. Be honest with yourself and open up more of your potential to become the future leader and success you desire. This process is about you discovering clarity to make a difference and create real value for those around you. You may find the most important nuggets you write down have nothing to do with what you are reading. Don't judge this. There's no "wrong way." Just record your thoughts and begin. Be open to the promptings that come from embracing your uniqueness and acting on what you really want in life.

Investing time to answer these questions begins your growth immediately! As you return later to what you wrote, you'll see evidence of your progress. Tangible encouragement. Reviewing your progress will give you a sense of satisfaction if you're concerned the development is taking too long. You can then look to see how far you have already come because you have something physical to review—your journal. Ultimately, if we are successful together on our journey, you will become your best friend, mentor and cheerleader. You have everything you need within you. I believe God placed it there alongside the spark of life as you were created. Now it's up to you to decide to be the best you; take action toward it. There's no one else on the planet with your uniqueness, your thumbprint or the ability to fully realize your divine purpose.

Let's talk about why you are where you are. Often, where you are is a place you've gotten to and accepted based on thinking that isn't completely true, that's limiting, and negativity you can free yourself from as soon as you're aware it exists.

This process may seem elementary. You may think you've heard this before. I invite you to remain open. It's not whether or not this information is new to you that matters. What matters most is that you are open to the wisdom and ready to take action to apply this to help you realize your success now. So many smart people hold themselves back making quick comments like, "I know!" or "I know that!" They block progress by looking smart instead of putting wisdom in action to create success. They are quick to bat back with their knowingness instead of listening to absorb a possibility or suggestion to create results for themselves right now.

Let's build our future success on a firm foundation. This is our most important investment, and one that pays off. As the old adage taught, "Well begun is half done." Engaging in this process, you'll be catapulted ahead. Catapult is pure momentum; you'll want to get that working for you right from the start. I can't overemphasize the value of starting right, to avoid having to stop later and start over. As you engage in a simple sequence of steps that creates the results you want, you can repeat this sequence and teach others to follow this same success pattern. Keeping things simple and making a repeatable process will make the work easier for you and those you lead.

You're on your way already to making a big difference in your life and those lives around you as you engage in this journey. You are not alone; I'm here to help you take the next step. Claim your power and embrace who you were created to be!

Let's start in your current situation, with a little theory that will help begin to light your new path.

Know A Crab When You See One

You may have heard of the Crab Theory. If not, it goes like this: If you have one crab you need a lid to keep that crab in the bucket. If you have more than one crab, you don't need a lid… that's because a crab with the ambition to escape will be pulled back down by the others.

What is this bucket? Let's call it our normal. It's what you've accepted as your normal life. The other crabs are the negative thoughts and negative situations we have accepted in our normal. We have dreams beyond the bucket and they become identified as, "that'll never happen!" We accept being pulled down by the crabs. You might see this acceptance in simple things like not voicing your opinions, or always putting yourself last, or not pursuing certain things because you already accept defeat. It's subtle. Your excitement for dreaming and exploring is being rationalized and discouraged by those who love you. They drown your bubbles of inspiration all in the name of helping you not get your hopes up or protecting you from failure. It's safe in the bucket, it's where everyone else is too. This life in the bucket is what you've settled for. It's not *that* bad anyway, right?

Until now you may not have known this bucket and the other crabs exist. It's a situation comprised of conditioned conclusions that prove you're not capable of achieving. Just the thought that the bucket exists brings a new perspective to your reality—your normal. Think of how many decisions you didn't actively make to get here in life. You avoided your genuine self and now you're in the middle of a bucket with lots of crab discouragement, pulling you down as you try to crawl out for something else. They're watching to see if you are making a run for it and trying to leave the safety normalcy.

As you begin to experience fulfillment by fully seeing yourself and your abilities, you'll see how your ambition to escape the bucket attracts even more people who want to pull you down. They're also stuck in a limited mindset you're climbing out of and they see the world through a limited lens. And don't be surprised if it's the people closest to you who express their love by trying to protect you and keep you safe from risk and failure— but also fulfillment. You might hear some disbelief from a friend or spouse about your capability to do anything new or different. It's normal to fear change. It's normal to play it safe. It's normal to choose caution instead of potential. You are now realizing the bucket you are in, so you can find your way out without being pulled down. You are pursuing fulfillment and that is a very different path. This is why it's important to stick to your convictions, work with yourself to see the crabs for what and who they are, and stay free to be more, so you can be genuine, climb freely and to eventually overflow.

 JOURNAL MOMENT

You're hearing the crabs right now, aren't you? Go ahead and give them a little room to speak their minds. What crabs do you hear and what are they saying that might limit your success? Writing this down does not give the negativity power. It calls it out! As you become aware of these things, you can choose to not allow them to stop you. You can work to reframe. After you've written down the negatives and limits, go back and examine each one. Maybe not right now… come back to these. Right now is about identifying the crabs. We'll deal with them head on in the coming chapters.

NOTE: It's important to note that this journal work is a continual spiral into discovering you. In the back of this book, you'll find a Lifeometer. It's a list of select questions from each chapter, so you can come back to them in a few months to answer. You'll have a new perspective when you look at these again and the new you that answers these questions will encourage and inspire. Looking back to see how far you've come is important on any journey. This reflection will help you realize just how far you've progressed as you've learned to let life flow. Don't be surprised at how quickly you've transformed.

Thanks Crab!

I have a great memory of one of my own bucket crabs and how it did me a huge favor. While I was in college, working as a waitress, a customer discovered I was majoring in graphic design just like she had years before. She immediately made her "crabhood" known by shamelessly dooming me snarling, "I hope you like being a waitress because you'll be one the rest of your life! I'm a graphic designer and I can't make any money at it!" Thankfully, my shock and anger froze me, or I'd have thrown her plate right in her lap!

I reframed her comments as a challenge. I had to. There were achievements to be had. I got a raise, got a better job, started my own business and momentum picked up. I saw my illustrations published in a children's book series, gained consulting clients and spoke in front of large audiences—I thought of her and how

I was glad to prove her wrong! Now imagine if I had taken what she said to heart, allowing her to influence my life with hers. At that time, I hadn't really stopped to consider what I truly wanted. I just knew what I didn't want. I knew who I wasn't. I wasn't her. She had her life and I had mine. I wouldn't fail as she had. If proving someone wrong can be such a fuel to success, what could proving to yourself that you are unlimited, great and powerful lead to?

 JOURNAL MOMENT

Now go back and visit with your crabs again. Let's shift your perspective to gain better understanding. Can you receive their comments as evidence of their concern and love for you? Are they afraid they won't fit into your new life if you succeed? Are they afraid you'll leave them behind? Are they disappointed in their own lives and want to keep you trapped with them? Can you find ways to involve them in your development, or will you do better by keeping them out of your bucket? If continuing in a relationship with them as you go for what you want, how will you set healthy personal boundaries to keep their negativity from infecting you? Will you limit the knowledge they have of your progress? Will you set certain conversations as off limits with them? Will you limit access or frequency of interacting with them to keep focused and maintain your progress? Remember, you are in charge of you! No one can make you less of you unless you give them the power to do so.

Sneaky Crab

So, the crabs aren't just other people. That's right, some of them live in your own head. Congratulations! You're normal. When the other crabs get talking, the crab inside your head is nodding. Sometimes, without encouragement the crab talks.

Albert Einstein said, "Insanity is doing the same thing, expecting different results." The corollary is, "If you always do what you've always done, you'll always get what you've always gotten." In order to break the cycle, we'll need to change the way we think, what we do, and what we believe we can have. We'll have to watch out for the limiting beliefs and all of the places where we believe we don't deserve love or success.

 JOURNAL MOMENT

Listen to how you think and speak. Are the words you use empowering or diminishing? Let's take a look at what you're telling yourself now that effects your fulfillment. Are you speaking what you don't want? Start paying attention to what you say about yourself and your business to others. That's more obvious than our thoughts, so we'll start there. Add to your list as you notice more false beliefs you can revise. Write them down so you can rewrite a powerful statement to take away any power these negative influences have over you. Your words do have power. They create your reality so becoming aware is the first step and rewriting them to practice empowering words is a great follow up to put action toward creating your future success.

They Aren't All Crabs

It's important to understand this doesn't mean everyone is a downer and you should close your ears and "la la la la la" your way forward. There are good influences too! And the way you respond to positive input is just as important as the way you respond to negative input. Listen to what people say when they talk about you. When they give you a compliment do you accept it as a gift, as truth, every time? Do you feel the need to return their compliment, like you owe them something?

I realized I was refusing the gift by not receiving their compliment. The value of relationship exchange is a two-way direction of both giving and receiving. This taught me how giving and receiving work together.

Now, maybe you feel your best when you're the one spreading positive input to others and that's fulfilling for you. I was like this too… here's something to consider. I met a person who revealed something very powerful that changed me forever.

I once met a lady who brought to my attention that if I wouldn't receive the gift of her compliment genuinely, I was ripping her off from the joy of giving! At first, I couldn't comprehend the true gift she was trying to give me. I would brush off a compliment and unknowingly completely diminish its empowering effect. Imagine someone complimented my outfit and I said, "This old thing? I've had this for years." Many of us are taught to be humble, to allow others to go before us, to not ask for things. This makes us think it's appropriate to deflect the gifts, compliments, confirmations, and acknowledgments that are ours to receive and own. This lady shared how rude it was of me to not accept her compliment. I was stealing away her joy of giving to me by not receiving her gift fully. This resonated with me also because I don't want to be rude.

I didn't want to "steal away anyone's joy of giving." Because of my mindset, I was building a wall around me, not allowing anyone to penetrate it. I only intended to be strong and not require people's help or compliments. This was a transformative moment for me. I would never be the same again. I got it! I not only completely received the gift of her compliment, I got the life lesson of how giving and receiving really works. It's powerful and it's worth catching your conditioned behavior to try to be humble and shift to receiving fully as others contribute to your life. As I became more open to receive, my life was enriched tremendously and the quality of my relationships improved substantially! Let people experience the full joy of giving and learn to become a great and powerful receiver. I bet your life will be forever transformed just by this one shift. Now imagine as you embrace this journey with me through this work and put The LIFE Process to work starting right now.

Really notice if you are open to receiving. Instead of saying a canned, "Thank you," say, "I receive that!" Hold back the urge to give a quick compliment back. No, it's not rude. You can always compliment the giver at another time when it's more genuine. Right now it's most important for you to retrain these automatic responses that diminish the powerful gift people are giving you. Another mentor of mine suggests to embrace the compliment by saying, "Thank you. I like hearing that. Can you tell me more?" If someone compliments you generally, don't hesitate to ask what they mean specifically, or to give you an example. That gives their compliment more depth and you more clarity. Then listen and immerse yourself in truly receiving their appreciation. See clearly how people appreciate you.

Commit to this change, don't *try* to do it—do it. This will change your behavior from a knee-jerk reaction, to consciously receiving. Your heart will absorb the compliment and you'll feel the love they intended. It's ok if this makes you emotional. Practice receiving love and you'll be strengthened.

Work to give compliments—remember, they're gifts—that you sincerely want to give. This is where you start to feel the power of being genuine with not just yourself, but others. My birthday is on Christmas so gift-giving practices always fascinated me. It saddens me to see someone give a gift simply because someone gave them a gift. If you weren't planning on getting that person a gift in the first place, then accept their generosity, receive their gift and thoughtfulness and in return give them the gift of receiving their gesture without obligation.

You can carry the spirit of gift-giving into any other day of the year where an unexpected gift will have even more impact if it is given sincerely. This works with gifts or compliments interchangeably. If you want to increase your ability to relate to people, seek to give sincere compliments more freely and deliberately. You'll be amazed at the response you'll get. As Dale Carnegie puts it in his book *How To Win Friends And Influence People,* "people are starved for appreciation."

Now that you've begun to think this way about yourself, about others, about your life… it's time for a big question.

WHAT
DO YOU WANT?

WHAT DO YOU WANT?

One time over lunch, a person asked me, "What do you want?" and I was caught completely off guard. I had my small talk recordings all cued up in my head and those all went right in the trash. At that moment, a simple question was like an arrow shot straight through my heart. I was stunned because I realized I had no answer. I had owned several businesses and experienced many successes, but it was in this moment I realized I hadn't stopped to consider what I really wanted—for me, for my life. To my surprise, emotion welled up inside me and I actually began to tear. Now embarrassment added to the flood of emotions. Ugh, how uncomfortable I was sitting there crying in response to such a simple question and in front of someone I hardly knew!

As I gathered my thoughts and emotions, I realized I had been reactive, not proactive, for such a long time. I'd felt a sense of accomplishment before, but I knew it was time for a change in direction for my life. I simply had not taken the time to reflect and explore what direction I wanted to go. I had not given myself the freedom to choose a new direction. This one simple question had a huge impact on my future. My natural response was a big clue that my divine calling was bubbling up inside of me. It was time to take notice of my gifts and talents and set course to achieve my purpose. From that moment I set out to fully answer that question and embrace whatever it held for me.

So now it's your turn…What do YOU want? Notice I didn't ask, "What do you deserve?" I ask openly, with no reservation, "What do you REALLY want?"

How does it feel to be asked what you want? Do you believe it's even possible to have what you really want? In a moment I'll ask you to write down your thoughts. This book is for you to learn and practice to set your heart free, think deeply, and write furiously.

You've already begun to think a little differently about yourself. Keep that going. What are the new things you allow yourself to see as the real you emerges and leads you to your destiny? Capture everything in your journal. The real you is breaking through and has the answer to this question "What do YOU REALLY want?" And the answers to so many other questions that will lead you on the path to a fulfilling life.

If you aren't steering your life, you're left to drift to places you may not want to go. You are the driver. You choose where to steer and the journey begins with knowing what you really want. Without knowing this, we'd have no idea of what direction to head causing us to lose time as we wander aimlessly. No one has time to waste!

We will begin right now by forming a strong foundation for you to let your life flow effortlessly. Take your time with each of these sections to really study how you're responding to these ideas.

 JOURNAL MOMENT

Now it's your turn. What do you really want? Take a moment right now to journal your thoughts and begin to steer or correct the direction of your own life. This is not the time to judge how you'll get there, or if what you want is possible. If those logical thoughts bubble up, just thank your inner crabs for any negativity or uncertainty. They are doing their job well! This inner voice is many times a reflection of your subconscious beliefs, conditioned patterning over time, and they are meant to keep you safe. Safe from change. Safe from your unlimited effortless life. Focus and allow the creator within you to work. Give expression to what you really want now. Capture this in your journal and verbalize it out loud if you dare.

What direction do you want to steer your life? Are you steering at all right now? Be open to ask the question and let your answer flow freely. If it takes time, that's okay. I have a business mentor who taught me, "Ask the question and the answer will follow." So if you can put it out there, you'll see that images and ideas will come to you as this universal principle plays out. The answer will come. Your answer. Your role is to ask the question and continue to ask better questions as you refine your development. Give yourself time and the answer will come to you and your path will be more obvious.

How Are You Doing, Now?

Together, we've brought some new perspective to your life. Do you feel hesitation? Do you feel stuck? Are you excited? Right now it's important to trust this process and learn to better trust yourself. As we have openness and understanding, we can move ahead to continue to make positive changes.

Shifting to a life of fulfillment takes preparation. Unfortunately, many are so eager for success that they get stuck being busy without making sure their activities lend a positive result. Success leaves predictable patterns, and successful people don't skip necessary steps.

Learning the importance of sequencing and focus is critical. Imagine baking bread and impatiently skipping the step of allowing the dough proper time to rise. Any missed step in a recipe causes a different potentially undesired result. Following the recipe will create a consistent outcome. Consider allowing some time to let the content of this book settle with you. Don't overlook something that appears simple and think it's not important. I find simple wisdom is the most profound and impactful. And I see many people miss important ideas while looking for complex ones.

We seem to plan details and miss the big vision. Why is it so many don't put the same attention into career or business preparation? Allowing even the briefest of focus on assessing your needs and focusing your actions will allow you to shave off many months and perhaps undesired paths or distractions. As we plan to succeed, success becomes our claim.

Change is hard, even when it's for the better. When it's happening, you don't realize what's on the other side. I remember reading Michael Gerber's *E-Myth Revisited* book just a few years into owning my first business. People kept recommending the book to me for more than a year, but I was too busy in my new business and never prioritized reading the book. Truthfully, I wasn't ready for the efficiency his book would deliver to my business, but I didn't know that at the time. When I finally did read the book, I learned a lot and reflected on the choices I had made in my business in that first year that had cost me. Now don't get me wrong. I had successfully left a substantial corporate salary, launched my own branding and marketing business, and tripled my income! Reading his book I saw that his wisdom in systematizing your operation could have made my success even bigger! Then as I became too busy again, I stopped reading the book just short of finishing it. When I returned months later, I found I had left off exactly where I was in the development of my business at that time. If I had finished the book months earlier, I could have avoided some challenges that I had just faced as I put the book down unfinished. I didn't avoid receiving the wisdom consciously. I just wasn't ready for the wisdom from that book until I was ready. I wanted to share this story with you to show you how your actions will reflect exactly where you are. When you are ready, you're ready!

To keep the momentum we're building, it may take a little more processing time to create a safe space and let go of fear. To help you work toward that place, we'll do an exercise with what we've learned so far that will strengthen you.

 JOURNAL MOMENT

Imagine what could be possible if you treated yourself with care and tenderness. Many of the people I meet admit that they are not their own best friends. Many times, we become our worst enemies. How are you treating yourself? Would you treat any friends or acquaintances the way you treat yourself? Would they still be your friend if you did?

Are you ready to move forward, or do you need to spend a little more time addressing the topics we've already mentioned? How would you be different with yourself if you understood that any setbacks are part of the process of building strength and wisdom?

Someone taught me a long time ago that in every occurrence, you either learn or succeed—both are valuable!

What Are You Ready To Believe?

Ok, this is the first step in our strength exercises. It's about the pursuit of life outside the bucket. You're in the bucket now, but what's out there? This is the beginning of separating from what you've accepted as your normal. Don't shrink back. Don't get pulled down. Willfully change your thoughts to begin laying the foundation for many extraordinary things to become evident in your life.

There are people who have walked after their doctors said they never would walk again, and people who have accomplished the highest academic awards when society or intelligence tests told them they couldn't. What makes the difference between one who perseveres and one who settles? From what I've seen, limits are set by your own belief in what is possible. So knowing and growing your belief is key to fulfilling your destiny.

Humanity's interest and exploration of the power of thoughts date all the way back to foundational principles from the *Bible* and up to more recent personal development works like the film, *The Secret*. We understand now more than ever that we are what we think about. What we focus on grows. Believe it and then we see it. What you really want may be challenging for you to see or ever think of receiving, but it can be achieved. What you really want—real success—is available to each of us whether you believe it right now or not.

"It's MY business. It's MY business." Leading people to say these words in seminars over the years has never stopped being impactful. It's not just the words, it's the attitude behind them... the belief in them. Many times people don't own their power as a business owner. Many people avoid owning their own personal power. You shrinking does not serve the world. The world needs you to rise to realize your purpose.

A naturopathic doctor shared her wisdom about the power of our words that I want to share with you. We were working on her branding and positioning her business, and she talked about the importance of educating patients in a way that helps them take positive action toward improvement without labeling their condition. Because of the fact that when a person gets a disease diagnosis—a label—by a doctor, they immediately enhance their symptoms by as much as eighty percent, fully embodying the disease. Speak and then become that. If naming and claiming can work against us, then it has to be just as powerful to work *for* us. You speak and create your existence with your thoughts and words. This is why you need to prepare first by shifting your mindset to be positive.

Our words have power. Speaking out loud allows your ears to hear your voice. We create with our spoken word. Add action and you increase the effectiveness. There is something powerful about stepping into a firm affirmation. I've seen it in my seminars. You become accountable to reality, it's no longer just in your head. You can stand firm with your legs planted like deep roots as you state your powerful affirmation and grow. Then as you state the affirmation out loud confidently take a forward step as you repeat the affirmation again and again with your forward movement. This is a great way to verbally and physically shape your world. You convince yourself as you take each step creating the new belief as you practice owning your power. You are embodying the most genuine you, the you that pursues what you really want.

And don't skip thinking this works in our personal lives—not just business! A cancer survivor shared the secrets of her success. She set out each day to get better in every way. She thought it. She believed it. She said it verbally and saw these words as she took every step of every day until one day she was "better in every way!"

I encourage you to write your own affirmation. As a part of this exercise, create an "I am" statement. Spiritually, the words "I am" are very powerful. Anything you attach after those two words are confirming and creating your reality. For instance, we can use this negatively saying, "I am stupid" and we then confirm we want more stupid in our lives. Understand that the spoken word has the power to create or destroy because of the beliefs that drive them. Choose your words carefully. Use the power of the two words "I am" to create your powerful affirmation and see how it impacts your behavior. Watch the world around you organize to fulfill your clear affirmed order.

 JOURNAL MOMENT

What is your powerful affirmation? Keep this with you and state it out loud often so you can hear your own voice claiming your power. If you have any trouble thinking of positive affirmations for yourself, ask some of your closest friends and mentors what are your strengths. Have them share how wonderful you are and then you can pull from their words to create your affirmation. Review written compliments you've received and pull words from there.

Now that you're soaked in affirmation and you're armed with affirmations… Let's attack those crabs we talked about earlier. All those negative, nasty things they spoke into your life. Cross each one out and write a positive that overpowers it or a solution that addresses a weakness. This builds strength to defeat the crabs. There may be days when all you have to write down are the negatives or limits people keep warning you about. Be confident the day will come when you're ready to scratch through them with positive solutions. Eventually, this response will be built into you. Those crabs don't stand a chance!

THE LIFE PROCESS

THE LIFE PROCESS

You're ready! You've spent a lot of time talking to yourself discovering how you've held back the true you. I'm going to share with you this three-step process that came out of my Transformational Leadership workshops. It was divinely inspired and I feel gifted to me. I've conducted many of these workshops and each person went through the same process I'm sharing with you here. The results were remarkable and unique. Some people discovered themselves for the first time in their life. Some cried, some laughed. Some were amazed that something so simple could be so profound. Many reclaimed their personal power back after being limited by a past experience. Some found validation they'd been looking for most of their life. I am so pleased to get to share this with you. So pleased that you have sought out this book and are here right now. I know it will be just as effective for you now where you are reading this if you let it.

Let's start moving forward with what you've found. It's time to fulfill up! Here is the three-part process we'll engage with shortly:

1. Believe

2. Decide

3. Act

But first, we need a little preparation.

I'll outline for you what you'll accomplish in each part. I'll continue to share my experiences as examples to clarify the key ideas and keep your imagination open and thinking focused. I recommend that you read through them all completely, and then go back and take it step by step, doing the exercises thoughtfully. See your blind spots. Capture this in your journal. Realizations like these tend to disappear as fast as you uncover them so your writings will help you follow the sequence and complete the transformation. As you review your writings over and over, you may see layers peeling back revealing a new clarity. I've had participants review their notes from this process months later to discover more revelations as they experience fulfillment and begin to overflow.

Preparation: Shift Your Mindset

No skipping steps! Remember, just as we prepare the ingredients for a recipe, we need to prepare to engage with this process to be ready to receive the results. As you become more aware you naturally start the process of improving your life.

One of my previous clients is a distributor of energy management products and solutions. He shared a simple but profound fact with me. He said that people simply being aware of energy conservation, changed their behavior to be more responsible with their consumption. So if they had something like a different light switch that drew attention to the energy conservation commitment, people would automatically consider whether it was really necessary to turn on the light for that room if they just needed to quickly get something and leave. If a regular switch was there, the switch went unnoticed and didn't create behavior change. Since the energy conservation switch looked different, it interrupted the habit and initiated an energy consciousness behavior instead of the previous, wasteful behavior.

Awareness is a key step. If you're not aware, you can't make necessary changes for improvement. That's huge, isn't it? Awareness is the difference between being stuck where you are and being able to succeed. Our perspective, our normal, can blind us to many things. You've been working hard to see yourself and your beliefs about yourself and your life in the last few chapters. Good work. It's no easy task to go hunting in the dark corners. You'll find as you continue to think this way that some of your beliefs are so deeply rooted in your past and your identity, they may be hard to see at this point.

For me, a big belief was about working hard. I grew up in Virginia and Kentucky, with relatives in North Carolina and our family's perpetuating belief was that you had to work hard for your money. It was part of the culture transferred from generation to generation in this particular area. Every single dollar mattered and we were raised to settle and be happy with whatever work we had. (Can you tell my parents grew up in The Depression era?) From that came limiting beliefs… take what you can get; don't expect to become more. That certainly didn't give me a foundation of abundance, of living life beyond the bucket we were all living in.

The most I remember my father earning as a professor before he passed was $35,000 a year. So imagine the knee-jerk I felt when I began selling marketing packages totaling $30,000-60,000 in a single month. An interesting pattern appeared. I believed I was somehow not working hard enough for the sum of money I was making… it wasn't right. Subconsciously perhaps

I felt guilty making that much in that short of a time. I would sell bigger and bigger branding and marketing service packages. But then, when sales stacked up in one month, it would take me longer than normal to finish the work. Making that level of money in one month broke outside my mindset of money at that time and the limiting belief that "You have to work hard for your money" would sabotage me. I didn't even realize this was holding me back until much later. This was many years ago, but I can still remember how shocked I felt when I realized I was actually limiting myself.

I hope my story helps you evaluate where you are with your own limiting beliefs. You may not know these limits exist. I certainly didn't see mine as clearly as I do now. I've done extensive work on identifying them to remove their limitations. Being aware of what limits you is the first step in diffusing the power it has over you. These thoughts are more a part of who we are than the crabs. They aren't external; they're practically built in.

Your mind also wants to be right. It will do almost anything to prove your existing beliefs right. You've already lived and weighed and seen and concluded… that's how you got here right? As we prepare for success, we'll look at what comes up and prepare your mind and heart to receive the fulfillment you will have in the near future. As you adjust your mindset, you'll adjust your "heartset" too.

My goal is not to challenge your beliefs, this is about you challenging them. I want to make sure they are your beliefs and not something that doesn't serve you. You will decide what works for you—the YOU that you've worked to define more clearly in this book. I'm here to work with you to guide an honest dialogue with yourself so you can decide and stick to actions, thoughts and words that keep you moving in the right direction.

Aren't you glad you've been practicing your journal moments? The work you do here will make a profound difference in your ability to receive fulfillment and experience success. Taking time to write what comes to mind will allow you to come back and review your thoughts, see your growth and celebrate your wins.

JOURNAL MOMENT

- ❏ What limiting thoughts do you have?
- ❏ Is your mindset telling you that you have to work hard for money?
- ❏ Do you think you deserve success?
- ❏ What do you think about money?
- ❏ Can you see yourself being successful? Can that really happen in your family?
- ❏ Do you have enough time or money to invest in your success?
- ❏ Have you tried becoming a leader or building a business in the past?
- ❏ Do you believe anyone can be successful in owning a business?
- ❏ What stops you from moving ahead?
- ❏ What excuses are you thinking of right now?

These excuses hold the keys to you shifting your mindset and moving one step closer to your success now.

- ❏ Do you want to shift your mindset?

Think about the word *mindset*, and listen to the sound. Doesn't it sound stuck? Mind-set.

❏ Are you able to shift your mindset?

❏ Do you really want to shift to what will serve you better?

❏ Are you ready to begin right now?

You might be ready now, you might be ready later down the road. That's ok. Timing is right when it's right for you.

Money is the result of your building a fulfilling and successful career or business. If you have a limited mindset about money, you'll not be able to receive that and therefore you'll struggle with the things that produce it, like promotions, sales, team building and opportunities.

❏ Are you worth it?

Many people are not able to receive because they feel worthless. It's amazingly and sadly common. I've done plenty of work myself in this area. Don't worry if you find you have this limited mindset. You've identified it so that you can overcome limits and build strength. You're already on your way.

❏ Are you afraid of success?

❏ Can you honestly say to yourself in the mirror that you are worth the success you are striving for? (Go have a conversation with yourself in the mirror. Seriously!)

❏ What do you think about success?

❏ Do you have a prejudice against successful people? Do you think they have it easy?

❏ What do you define as success for you?

❏ How do you imagine you will be when you are successful?

❑ Can you see your genuine self as a success?

❑ Are you building momentum to produce more success in your life and business?

❑ Are you ready to receive success?

❑ Think of fulfillment as a gift box that I'm presenting to you. Will you put out your arms and receive it right now?

❑ Do stories and judgments or other deflections come into your mind as I hold out this gift to you?

❑ Are you your best friend or worst enemy?

❑ What are you reading, looking at and thinking about? Remember what you focus on expands.

❑ How do you see yourself?

❑ Do you make jokes that belittle you?

Congratulations! You've done some heavy lifting to prepare—recognizing and shifting your mindset to receive fulfillment is no small feat. Now it's time to believe, decide and act.

You've created basic awareness and perhaps you've written your observations in your journal to get deeper into development in these areas. This work can have a great impact on your current situation and lead you to accelerate success. Review these three simple steps:

The LIFE Process

1. Believe

2. Decide

3. Act

As you complete these three steps, remember to take your leadership to the next level and explore the next level of belief, decisions and actions that need to be taken. It's not just about business, you can apply this sequence to your personal life as well. Always prepare by checking for limits in your mindset. Then build positive belief to create a strong foundation. Decide on your direction and goal. Then take immediate action to create your reality.

Create a positive impact in your community and the world by teaching this to people that you know and care about. Review this process often and share it with those ready to take action as you have. You'll be amazed at how following simple steps will put you on your path to reach success. The questions will uncover your inner greatness and shine light on your chains of limit. Be kind to yourself. As you learn to become your best friend, turn the inner crab into your coach and mentor, you'll see you are capable of more than you first imagined.

These simple steps, one by one, when followed get you to what you want—fulfillment and your success. As you achieve and grow more and more, others will look to you to lead them to do the preparation you did and want you to guide them step-by-step to their own success. Open your eyes to see who is around you. Remember to just see and hear them. You'll discover the same calling that I did. People just need to be seen and heard. Then as you teach them to receive the life they have already been given, assist those willing to receive success as they let it flow effortlessly into all areas of their existence.

1. Believe

"I believe it's possible." This was always one of my favorite comments to hear from people as they completed a training exercise that I lead for direct sellers and network marketing leaders. They were able to arrive at this statement through simulated practice of how their business worked. It took less time to transfer experience through simulation and at the end of the session, they had built genuine belief and practiced how to complete the daily activities necessary for success in their business.

Here's what a scenario for a direct selling or network marketing business looks like: Many hours and multiple meetings had gone into trying to convince a new distributor what's possible with this type of business model. The leader may have noticed the prospect's body language as being engaged, leaning forward, head nodding and eyes open wide as the prospect seemed to be listening. The leader felt confident that the connection was being made and that this new business owner was ready to go to the moon like a rocket.

What couldn't be seen was the mindset and negative self-talk going on behind the curtain of his face—the silent business-killer thoughts like, "Loser, don't think this can happen to you. It's only for this guy or gal who has it made already since he/she's from the corporate office. You'll never make it in this. This is going to be just like that thing your relative got you into five years ago. This is a waste of time. You've got bills to pay. Why don't you get a real job and make some money to pay for groceries?" Our minds have practiced being negative and many have become so good at holding themselves back that they don't even know they are doing this to themselves. They disguise limiting beliefs as logic.

Seeing this over and over again I learned that belief is a foundation. It needs to exist to be built upon. We can't develop anything that we don't believe. That's why it is the first step in this process. I had a belief when I was in college that I would be successful as a graphic designer. As I left the corporate world and started my own business, I believed I could be successful as an entrepreneur. I built this belief over the year working my business part time before I made the jump from corporate to full time entrepreneur. We are able to borrow another person's belief in our ability, but to have long-lasting fulfillment, you'll want to build a strong foundation of your own belief. That's how you're going to meet the challenges that come along the way.

In the transformation of a butterfly, you can't interfere with the process. You can't reduce the struggle as the butterfly comes out of the cocoon. The squeezing has a purpose, it's pushing fluid into the wings so the butterfly can fly. Our role as leaders is to inspire people to do their own work and find their own fulfillment—that's how they succeed. We are called to love and encourage them sincerely, through a difficult process. We support their transformation and development, but they must own the activities and do the work themselves. We might offer suggested learning, clarify understanding, encourage action and suggest focus. And remember that a flutter of a butterfly's wings can be felt in ripple effect air movement all over the world. So don't be judgmental of how little your accomplishment might be. Any movement in the direction of realizing your greatness is positive movement; even the smallest progress is important.

Hearing other people's stories can be inspiring but always keep in mind they are just that—other people's stories. It can also set the bar out of reach, setting up the new person to compare and compete against other people. You've seen it in crowds where there is a prize or drawing of some kind. People will blurt out, "Oh, I never win." And, guess what? They don't. They begin things already defeated. You cannot go any further in reality than your mind can believe. The key is to build our belief and celebrate as we grow.

Imagine blowing up a balloon. As you let the air out, the balloon cannot return completely to its original size. Learning is powerful because it increases your capacity as we continue. You need to build belief so you can achieve a higher level of success. Belief is stretched or expanded by your education and personal experiences and allows you to become a bigger person—someone with big presence, big goals, big impact. You have to have courage to take action and when you do the positive results fuel the belief you're building. That's why encouragement and support accelerates development. Notice any type of sports coaching where they continue to support the athlete to increase their ability a step at a time. Belief instilled with actions builds your world. These actions build confidence in you and practicing this new-found confidence grows the belief.

Now, commit to your belief. Make sure you believe in what you are working toward and that you have confidence in the unique gifts you have to share. You'll be amazed at what you can accomplish when you build belief and commit!

After illustrating a series of children's books, I'd cringe when I was incorrectly introduced as the "author," and say I was "just the illustrator." Yes, I was the illustrator, but I allowed myself to feel less than. For years, I hesitated to embrace my dream of writing books. Do you ever label or limit yourself that way? Watch out for sneaky ways you diminish your power or accomplishments. This erodes your momentum. Then one time a woman was looking through one of these children's books and she stopped, putting both of her hands on the opened book. She took a deep breath, a big smile stretched across her face, her eyes lit up and she looked right at me and declared, "This is what I imagine God's love looks like. I can feel it." It was the most amazing compliment I've ever received. She felt exactly what God had inspired in me to create in that work. I received her compliment fully and understood how important my contribution was to that project. I owned the accomplishment. I didn't have to be the author at that point in my life. I created something valuable, something real with my talent.

Watch for labels in your life that limit you—the ways you squeeze yourself down into a box. These labels don't serve us to be all we've been created to be. As you become aware of what's stopping you, take action to overcome this and you'll be ready to step up to another level.

> *"Once your thoughts reflect*
> *what you genuinely want to be,*
> *the appropriate emotions and*
> *the consequent behavior will flow automatically.*
> *Believe it, and you will see it!"*
> —Wayne Dyer

JOURNAL MOMENT

❑ What and who do you genuinely want to be?

❑ What would you do if you believed you couldn't fail?

❑ How would this change your actions today or tomorrow?

When people commit to play all out at a higher intensity than they have done before, massive change can happen and you can get momentum and excitement working for you.

Think and write about this right now: "Do you believe it is possible for you to succeed right now?"

❏   Can you let go of fear and plan for a day of intensity to build your business now? Try it for a day and then document what happens. See what results can be attained.

❏   How would you introduce your genuine self?

Write down an introduction of yourself, as the success you are, so someone else could introduce you to an audience. Successful people are often asked to speak and inspire others by sharing their wisdom. Share yours. Use as many descriptors to paint the picture of what your fulfilling life looks like and make it as real as you can see right now. You may want to post this on your bathroom mirror and put a copy in your wallet to carry with you. Put it right with your money so when you purchase anything you'll see your success and see you're valuable. Your words and thoughts have power. Use them to produce a powerful successful you. The more you believe in you, the more others will believe and see you as the success you are.

2. Decide

You cannot omit the "Decide" step from your journey. In fact, I believe this is the most important and missing step in many people's lives. If you choose not to make the decision, you are deciding not to move ahead. Napoleon Hill, author of *Think and Grow Rich,* discovered that one of the success principles is "to be decisive in nature." Decide to get ready for fulfillment.

Decide to welcome your ship as it comes in. Decide to succeed. You have the choice. Making that decision sets a course of actions. Not making that decision still determines a course of actions, just not the one you really want. This is when the actions toward your extraordinary life reveal your path to success. Your future fulfillment and success await you. They hinge on this moment, this decision.

Choose what you really want and you'll be amazed at what is possible. Choose no, and your life will remain mostly the same, though now you have awareness that you didn't have before. Decide your "why" for becoming successful to help you stay focused and motivated. The bigger your reason, the more force it has to keep you motivated and focused. Choose something with real gravity in your life.

I've worked with entrepreneurs, business owners and leaders for nearly thirty years. I see people get stuck when they don't plan their actions toward a goal. If we choose ahead of time the purpose will direct our activities. If I create a business just to cover my personal lifestyle or monthly expenses, I will become limited. This type of business will be nothing more than a job. I'll find myself always working never having freedom to allow the business to work without me, beyond me. Dreams and fulfillment aren't born out of necessity. Limiting them to bills suffocates potential. Don't just think about your needs, think beyond yourself. That's the type of business that you can set up to create passive income or even sell to someone else since it does not depend on you to operate it. The business meets a market that wants the solution the business provides. This market will continue to transact as long as they know the solution exists and they find value in buying what this business has to offer. If I decide to create a business that offers value to the world, beyond myself, and have a team of people working with me, there are no limits. In that scenario we are fulfilled, able to overflow and create real value for others.

Many people miss setting proper expectations and designing their business to have purpose. I've seen my own mistakes rooted in not setting a goal and deciding what actions to take toward it. I know you're ready to go, but be sure not to jump past good business principles no matter how passionate or impatient you are. There are good guides to planning a business that are there for a reason. Follow them! They are there to serve you so you can serve others.

Many people don't believe it's possible to have a business that gives them freedom. It's as if they can't see the possibility. It is possible. We are so brainwashed to work a job that many times we create our business from the limits of a job-worker instead of from an unlimited business owner. This is why identifying your real self and embodying the genuine *you* is so important. Decide who you are and how you act. Your intentions, action and purpose are critical to your future success. The key is to decide what you want, what type of lifestyle you want, and create the business profession that will bring you that result.

A key way to enhance your lifestyle is to help more people enhance theirs. Together everyone achieves more. It's teamwork. You are seeking to build success for yourself but not by yourself. It works so much better and faster when you work with people to build everyone's success together. Too many times we are lead to believe that cut-throat, dog-eat-dog is the way to get ahead… but I've seen a much different case.

You can create all kinds of teams. They can be strategic partners, service professionals, joint ventures, masterminds, associations, etc. Think of your team as a success network offering you the specific support you need to achieve your goals.

As I sat to decide what type of lifestyle I wanted, it became increasing clear that I wanted to mentor and lead a team of people who delivered value to the marketplace and helped change the world. I love meeting people and am sincerely interested in them and their story. I like to travel and speak to audiences and meet people for coffee to discover what they really want out of life.

Imagine my surprise when I found the best business model for my skills and desires was to build a network marketing business. In the past, I had incorrectly judged that this business model had limitations. But as I investigated the direct sales and network marketing industry, I realized the choice in the company, ownership, product and market need were very important to investigate before getting involved. It is critical to look at the company's intent, vision, and why. It's just as critical to evaluate the data of their customer retention rate (the industry is low double digits but companies exist with high seventy to eighty percent retention or more!), quality of the product or service distributed, evaluate the longevity of the business opportunity and the richness of the compensation plan.

I'm pleased to have found a company that I feel offers great opportunity as it solves important problems in both healthcare and building wealth. What I appreciate the most is the kind of leaders we attract and produce. Culture is important. If you don't like the product and don't fit the culture, it probably won't make you happy joining in a company just because it has a business opportunity available. It is this community of great and powerful but most importantly thoughtful leaders that I enjoy the most in my company choice. If it wasn't for deciding to build this network marketing organization, I would have never believed it could exist. Luckily, I had just enough belief to start and decide to go for it. And I haven't looked back since!

*"Within you right now is the power to do things
you never dreamed possible. This power becomes
available to you just as soon as you can change
your beliefs."*

-- Dr. Maxwell Maltz

JOURNAL MOMENT

❑ What is your why? Does it have a gravitational pull? Would you say it would be hard to ignore this calling, career or way of being?

❑ What direction are you deciding to go with your career?

❑ What is the purpose of your business?

❑ Why is this your focus? Why now?

Will you stick with your decision when it's uncomfortable? I could tell you that once you make the decision, it will be easy street from there on out. I haven't found that to be the case nor have I heard that from any mentors I have met along the way. Each of us runs into that breakthrough wall at different places and it impacts us with different intensities. Your story will emerge and like any legendary hero, you'll have hardships and become stronger in the end. Personally, I find the challenges confirm that I'm on the right path.

I've always loved the analogy of a silversmith's refinement. They put the raw metal into the fire to burn out the impurities. Do you know how they know when their metal is refined into pure silver? When the silversmith can see their own reflection in the molten metal. Once the material reflects its maker, it is pure! It is ready to be removed from the fire and shaped for the maker's purpose. How beautiful is that?

❑ Is now the right time for you?

❑ Do you have a clear focus? If not, you may need to spend some time to do this before you can be decisive.

Think on this: Listen to the word Decide. See it as "D"-side. The "D" could stand for different sides of your decision. Positive things like Divine side, or Delightful side. Negative sides like Defeated side, Defensive side, or Destroy side.

What inspiration have you received that you may not even have expressed out loud? For a moment don't think about all that you can't do or what you think you can't become. What are you talented at? What are your gifts? If you used all of your gifts and strengths what would you do?

Decide is a strong word that eliminates distractions as you decide and act upon that decision. Are you choosing from your divine inspiration side or are you reacting to your defeated side keeping you stuck and playing small? Decide will put you on one side or the other. It's your choice. Which D-side do you choose?

If it's time to make the decision, do it now. As you make decisions, make them quickly and change them over time. Avoid flipping back and forth or you may delay your progress appearing uncertain. Decide to receive success. If now is the time...

❑ What have you decided?

3. Act

My friend Rhonda, a top business leader, once said, "I learned..." and then she corrected herself saying, "Well, I haven't applied it yet, so I guess I haven't learned it!" Knowing is one thing; learning or doing something with the knowledge is something more. Applied learning is knowledge in motion. Nothing happens when you just know information. The Law of Attraction shares the rest of the secret right there within the word. AttrACTION. Put action to the wisdom you've learned to create results.

You've been preparing for your success here in the same way you prepare to build a house. You work the first stages below ground. You spend a lot of time digging, pouring footers and then the foundation appears. At first very little physical progress is visible, but you know you've done the work. Now it's time to keep moving toward what you really want. Time to translate all this information into results. Ask any builder or architect what would happen if you skip this preparation and they'll point to disaster or certainly a short lived building. It is the same with this preparation for fulfillment. Be patient with yourself as you create new thoughts and build strength to own your power. You want to get this right. You want to be ready.

We might not have seen you prepare by battling the bucket crabs, getting unstuck from a mindset or releasing limiting beliefs. This all happens inside. But the evidence of removing the mindset barrier appears as you are able to receive more money, more success or a larger organization as you build. Notice your language, it's telling of how you see yourself now. Is it getting stronger and can you hear your conviction? Do you feel your commitment to your success increasing?

We might not have witnessed you building your belief. But we might see that you're aware of your obstacles, tracking your goals and taking daily actions that are all built on a foundation of belief. Listen as you may be challenged to express what you believe is possible for you right now. Remember no one but you sets your limits. Believe and trust in your fulfillment and you will begin to see your success.

We might not have seen your decision being made, though now we can trace it back to a place where things shifted. Once at a retreat, I made the decision to stop being a human *doing* and be a human *being* and from that moment on, I became a more powerful human being. I did that by being genuine. It's the only version of you that can get where you want to go. As a human being, embracing my real self shifted me toward my real goals. I chose more strategic, big picture planning and less tactical, brass tacks projects. I developed my leadership capabilities because I wanted to play at a higher level in business and not be constantly tied to a computer doing the tasks. My focus shifted to understand people more as I knew this level of leadership meant I needed to inspire people with my knowledge and experience to help them take the next step and act to create their own success.

Take action and apply knowledge each day to get real results. It's key to be a constant learner. Feed your knowledge regularly and apply this to gain experience. Knowledge plus experience gives you great wisdom. Wisdom in action assures your success. The great shortcut is not to rely only on your own knowledge or experience. You can borrow wisdom from coaches, consultants, experts, leaders, mentors and speakers to accelerate your progress. Books like this one lift you to succeed on top of my experience that's transferred to you here. It's when you act on the wisdom you've gained that you create your success. Take action with what you know and gain experience to increase wisdom and your life will change. Remember the balloon? This will stretch you beyond where you were and you will be forever transformed.

> *"The only difference between success and failure is the ability to take action."*
> -- Alexander Graham Bell

JOURNAL MOMENT

We've just covered a lot of things. You've worked underground to prepare the dirt and pour the foundation of your success.

You understand the value of building belief, and learned how you can continually reinforce your own belief. As you made a decision to continue on and find yourself at this point in the book, now is the time for you to act.

- ❑ Write about the actions you're taking.
- ❑ What do you want to remember about what you've just read and how it applies to you now?
- ❑ Have you identified sources of wisdom you can tap into?
- ❑ What actions are you willing to commit to monthly, weekly or daily to progress toward realizing your goal?
- ❑ Are you taking action alone or do you need to form a group or team to work together to take action to bring you all to fulfillment?

Embrace Change & Uncertainty

Keep Climbing

On a rock climbing training exercise at a gym, I took it on with confidence. Then, as I surpassed my height comfort level—about the height of rooftops where I'd been before—my hands started sweating and my nerves got out of control. The little hand and foot hold bumps on the wall were getting smaller and harder to hold onto the higher I went up the wall. Thoughts rushed into my mind like, "If I fall, will the ropes hold me?" I doubted. I worried about how I'd get down. Then I imagined the embarrassment of not being able to make it to the top. And worse yet, I felt the pressure of others watching me. My head was loud with negatives so I couldn't even hear their positive coaching or encouragement.

How often do you worry about something two or three steps beyond where you are now? It's the "What if?" syndrome that stops many of us from progressing. You might find yourself there now. Tackling how you perceive yourself, your life and your future is not a small task. It's exciting to think about finally going for what you really want, but there will be moments of doubt and even fear once you make progress.

What started as simply uncomfortable feelings quickly turned to tangible fear. I found myself paralyzed on that rock climbing wall. I was unable to care about reaching my goal, and I had been so confident moments earlier as I stood on the ground—the top seemed further away from me now. I couldn't go any further until I felt what it was like to trust the ropes and know they would hold my weight. After much persuading, the coach let me come down, and the ropes actually held! All I had to do was walk down the wall surface, just like walking on the ground. As I got to the floor, my knees buckled weakened by the fear I'd been feeling; I could hardly stand upright. I was physically exhausted from my emotional defeat.

Then, knowing we just removed some major barriers, I didn't even unbuckle. I asked to go right back up. The lies I had often told myself were gone. They had no power over me. My experience gave me new confidence. Those exhausting negative emotions couldn't rule me anymore. As I hit the same challenging spot with those smaller hand and foot holds, I knew I had to keep my weight shifting back and forth from foot to foot. Stay in motion. This became my new gained tool. If I stopped, I knew my fear would paralyze me. I reached my goal of making it to the top and came back down feeling stronger than ever before. I had overcome fear, not allowed it to rule me, and I learned the power of moving even slightly to avoid being paralyzed. This exercise taught me valuable keys to overcoming fear in other areas of my life. How we do anything is how we do everything.

Some time ago I learned that fear and excitement are the exact same emotion. The difference is the interpretation and the label I assign to it. Our minds are amazing! Imagine two people riding a rollercoaster. One enjoys the thrill and the other is petrified fearing death. Use your mind to create positive experiences that move you ahead instead of paralyzing you and holding you back. Deal?

 JOURNAL MOMENT

When have you accomplished something that challenged your fears and previous limits? How will you overcome your limited thinking in the future? Are you okay to be uncomfortable to grow to where you need to be to create success in your life? Are you willing to do whatever it takes to push through challenges to break through to your success?

List any fears that you have right now. As you see these fears written down, evaluate if they are valid or true. If so, then what can you do to diminish the level of power they have over you? Working this out on paper can keep the emotion out of it. Much of the time, it's the emotion that fuels the fear. Thinking about this, especially ahead of time, allows you to plan a course of action to take before the fear gets a grip on you. Remember you have a choice. Notice the fears and decide if you want to do something about the power they have over you. You don't have to do anything you don't want to but you can see now that there may be a cost to letting a fear define or defeat you.

Change Is Constant

Our world is always changing. In fact, the only constant is change. Whether you're pursuing, like you are now, or it is happening around you… change is a part of living. Just listen to the stories from our elders as they comment on the price of bread or how their world was different with no television. You don't need to be a scientist to see the cycles of change as we mature. Ask any parent and we'll tell you that we're amazed at how fast our kids grow up. Ever owned a puppy or a kitten? Sometimes it feels like they change overnight!

Everything is in a constant state of flux. Some changes are so subtle, we don't really notice them until we stop and take notice. Other changes are dramatic. So why resist change? It's human nature to resist and fear change, the unknown. We fear that things will not be as good as they were. Or we like our routine so much, we may not be able to receive the gift of change for the better.

When we resist change, we paralyze ourselves, cause collisions and turn our lives upside down. Because in reality, we are growing and there is momentum in continuing to climb. Each new step, each change, when taken with purpose, will bring wonderful, positive new things into our lives. We have to create the interpretation that allows us to embrace change in our lives and not fear it.

As Zig Ziglar, says, "Fear is nothing more than False Evidence Appearing Real." We tell ourselves stories that keep us trapped right where we are, getting less than we want. What false stories do you believe? Remember the power of belief? This is the negative manifestation of that truth. How does having this fear, this story, serve you? Know that the fear is designed to protect us. Its goal is to keep us from moving into uncertainty and unknown. The problem comes when fear overpowers and begins to paralyze us from moving ahead. When the story becomes bigger than what is true, fear has got a hold of you. These are the times it's key to be decisive. Decide exactly where you want to go as you focus on taking steps toward success. Stick to your decision to help push through fears as they come up along the journey. Remember, this is all about what you really want. Not just covering your bills, not just taking what you can get. This is much more important.

> *"It is not the strongest species that survive,*
> *nor the most intelligent,*
> *but the ones most responsive to change."*
> – Charles Darwin

JOURNAL MOMENT

Which footholds are you looking forward to? Do you wish you could stay where you are? Who can help you raise your awareness of what is necessary for the success you desire? What false stories are you making up? Are you the type that continually looks to the past wishing it were like the good old days? There is only one moment that we live in and that's this present moment. The past is history and the future may not come.

Think of driving down the freeway. Where do you focus? Not on the rearview mirror or looking over your shoulder. You don't focus too far down the road in front of you either. Now think about the path you are on right now. What is right in front of you? Do you even know where this current path is leading you?

CREATE REAL
VALUE

CREATE REAL VALUE

In the classic movie, *It's a Wonderful Life*, Jimmy Stewart's character is so focused on his job, his responsibilities, his obligations, and what he makes or doesn't make, that he sees no point in living. He learns the value of his life was never about what he made; it was about what he made possible for everyone around him. He learns what a difference his presence has made. His life meant so much more than what he originally believed.

You have power available in you and to you. You've been working on discovering it, owning it and putting it into motion. You've seen staying in motion even slightly can overpower paralyzing fear. Now let's overflow to share our progress to benefit others.

In this section, we'll explore how powerful we really are and see how that translates into not just fulfillment for you, but into overflowing into the lives around us. When you're fulfilled, you have something endless and wonderful; you're a source and you can give to others in a way that impacts them tangibly. We'll explore the different types of value and exercise your new way of thinking, feeling and acting. Here's where the rubber meets the road.

You can choose to focus on things that are here today and gone tomorrow. You can assume your success is only about the products or services you sell. While useful at times, these are only the means. It's not about what we make that really matters. It's about what we make possible for the people in our lives. It's about the collaborative communities we build that become endless sources of continued development for all humankind. We are better together.

There is abundance here that is beyond comprehension. It flows from fulfillment. When one person wins, that doesn't mean others lose. There isn't just one winning position. You can have it any way you desire. Through the collaboration of humanity, we can conceive, become and achieve. There is more than enough to go around the world again and again—the ultimate resource.

We all have great worth and gifts to share with the world. The problem is that we've been tainted over time to forget or disbelieve this. I love the way Marianne Williamson put it. You might have heard it quoted in one of my favorite movies to watch with my kids, *Akeelah and the Bee*:

> *"Our deepest fear is not that we are inadequate. Our deepest fear is that we are powerful beyond measure. It is our light, not our darkness that most frightens us. We ask ourselves, who am I to be brilliant, gorgeous, talented, and fabulous? Actually, who are you not to be? You are a child of God. Your playing small does not serve the world. There is nothing enlightened about shrinking so that other people won't feel insecure around you. We are all meant to shine, as children do. We were born to make manifest the glory of God that is within us. It's not just in some of us; it's in everyone. And as we let our own light shine, we unconsciously give other people permission to*

*do the same. As we are liberated from our own fear, our
presence automatically liberates others."*

Maybe right now, you're hearing a whisper I've heard before: "You're playing too small." Maybe you even fear you are too small to make any real difference. What purpose do we accomplish when we belittle ourselves or shy away from our real power? It's our sneaky way of taking ourselves out of the game. We play small because we think small serves us or that we don't deserve to play big. Perhaps we misunderstand humility and think it will be better to shrink than appear prideful. Clearly when we take this approach, we don't believe in what's possible for us at that moment. We push the gift of success off to someday in the future, or we drown the hope of ever being a success.

As I first encountered Marianne Williamson's quote, I sensed deep in my soul that I was playing too small. Now at that time, I was a graphic designer and I owned a branding and marketing firm in the Phoenix, Arizona metro area. I had made a bold jump from working a corporate job to owning my own successful business. In addition, I had even invested my resources to design and illustrate a children's book series that created another separate business with the author of the series. Even with these accomplishments evident, as I first read that quote a whisper inside invited me to explore that there was something even bigger and more fulfilling. Something specific to me and my gifts.

Deep down, I knew I could inspire more people to take action to embrace their own uniqueness and be all they were created to be. I knew I was being called to serve more people, and yet, I didn't have the slightest idea how that would come about. I hadn't paid much attention to the responses people had continually shared with me that they felt better being around me and that they loved listening to me share encouragement to them about their unlimited abilities. But somehow hearing this quote sparked this future that I could not yet see. Did I dare believe it could be true? Could my presence alone be enough? Could I make my livelihood doing the one thing I really loved—meeting, listening and speaking with interesting people?

I had been blessed to achieve many things and produce a great income to support my family. I had wanted more freedom and the types of businesses I had at this time were consuming my time, increasing my stress, and not expanding my choices or freedom. I had adapted to the level of stress from this profession, but I knew it was not the best for my health. I knew it was time to leave the graphic design profession, but I had no idea what was next. I kept hearing that small whisper, "You're playing too small." It was an invitation I had to embrace.

I have a team of people that I turn to for advice. Many of these people could be considered to be my competition, but I see them as priceless allies. Since we understand the same challenges, we can help one another shortcut the process. The dialogue is just as beneficial for both of us as we seek to create the most value in our lives and businesses. It's what I like to refer to as Collective Intelligence. When many come together, the sum is more impactful than the individual parts. We enhance and multiply what each of us knows individually. Our unique strengths fill in a more complete whole than any one individual. It's the secret to the power of a group organized for a cause. It becomes powerful on its own. This isn't about reinventing the wheel, it's about being a part of the change to a world that is shifting into more collaboration. It really does start with you.

My good friend and mentor, Sharon Lechter demonstrates this in the equation: $1 + 1 = 11$. As she holds up one finger on each hand and moves the two hands together you get the impact of our coming together. It's a great visual to show the value of relationships. Reading Sharon's book, *Three Feet From Gold*, you can explore more on the power of having mentors, sharing wisdom and collaborating.

Joint ventures and the power of collaboration are powerful and they can accelerate your accomplishments. You may have heard it said, "Two heads are better than one." As you strive to let your life flow effortlessly to make a difference, you'll want to learn more about creating win-win relationships. No one gets to the top alone. When you create overflow, you don't focus on loss. There's more than enough to spare. In this abundance mentality, you'll find that people are really interested in your success and they will be generous with wisdom and contacts the same way you have been with them.

Collaboration will become more important in the coming years. Sure competition creates a necessary tension that can lead to new advancements and innovation, but when there is inherent win-lose programming, you'll miss realizing your fullest potential in this old paradigm. As you embrace creating win-win situations, your results are multiplied exponentially. Instead of viewing people as your competition, seek to find ways to form mutually beneficial relationships. We call it board of directors, power partners, or power table in business. There are increased market shares and profits to be realized as you fully embrace an age of collaboration.

JOURNAL MOMENT

So what do we make possible? What difference do you want to make? What can you see so far? Celebrate how wonderful your life is and think about yourself in that movie. What events are you proud to have contributed to? What do you wish you could have contributed to? Who can you seek out for advice, counsel, or mentorship? Is there someone that you could go and apprentice with to gain more understanding about your purpose? Can you identify people that can benefit in a win-win relationship with you or your company?

The Value of Learning

A friend of mine worked in the medical industry. She shared with me their philosophy for duplicating learning. "See one. Do one. Teach one." It's a great formula for distributing knowledge and experience to rapidly deploy the entire community. The first step is to observe the teacher or mentor. Then you engage in doing the activity yourself. Then to make the learning stick, you teach someone else who observes you. This is how you get duplication working to share the learning rapidly and effectively.

I utilize this daily in my leadership organization. I have observed, done and taught to master the skills needed in my profession. I let my colleagues observe how to invite people to learn about our products. As they report on doing their own invitations, I offer questions and suggestions for them to learn from doing the actions needed to build their organization. Then as they become accomplished at attracting people who want to learn and use our products, their skill is refined as they teach others what they've just learned. It's simple and the development can go as fast and far as they can imagine. That's why it's so critical to work on your inner belief and know what you've decided first so you don't set limits on your actions.

My desire for knowledge and inquisitive awareness allows me to learn from everywhere. I'm fascinated by learning. I'm interested in people. If you're open to it, every situation offers clues and meaning. My youngest daughter likes to remind me to take breaks from my life of learning as she says, "everything and every situation doesn't have to mean something!" Rightfully so, she demands a break from her mom giving a perpetual personal development or leadership seminar. And I'm learning from her that even though I love my work, it's best for me to sometimes just live life and not over evaluate everything to find the meaning.

I believe those who are set in their ways or believe they have learned everything will have a much harder time adapting to the culture shift we are in. They also have built a fence of limiting beliefs around themselves that prevent them from experiencing real fulfillment. I think a person's ability to learn directly correlates to their inner confidence. I know who I am and what value I bring to my community, so I can be open to learning new things and seeing knowledge as way to become even better.

As we have a shift in business, organizations need to rapidly retrain and lead people to learn new things. Entrepreneurs and small businesses have an advantage that they are nimble and can quickly deploy new learning. Corporations will need to utilize this type of powerful training to stay on top of change. Great leaders inspire learning in their organizations. Great ideas and solutions can come from any level within the organization.

You may have heard that practice makes perfect. But learning doesn't mean obsessive practice. Imagine if I continue to model the same ineffective action over and over. This would satisfy as practice, but the result would be the same ineffective result. Perhaps it's better stated as perfect practice makes perfect. The emphasis needs to be on the source of origination. You can ask, "Is what I am modeling effective to solve the problem?" And, "Is what I'm doing worth repeating and duplicating?" You'll know the answer as you want to duplicate the results. Results don't lie.

It's this reason I use the word learning and not training. I facilitate learning. Training relates to teaching as learning relates to mentoring. Teaching tells and mentoring compels. To tell is to push. To compel is to pull and actively involves you. As I'm expanding to lead teams of thousands and tens of thousands in my organization, telling my leaders how to be doesn't work. I must compel them to do the inner work, to learn their destiny. I match their energy as they progress. I am available for mentoring but if they aren't asking for my guidance, it's best to hold my suggestions until they ask a question. Their questioning shows they are ready and open to developing how to go to the next level in their leadership. I already believe in them more than they do. It's best to let them discover and grow their own belief to create a long lasting committed leadership partnership.

It can be difficult to allow your colleagues and relationships the necessary development time to be open to this transformation, but imagine the satisfaction of becoming the best leader you can be, and then leading others to become their best. Can you see a community of great and powerful leaders collaborating to make a difference in this world? I do. It's a beautiful process. Everyone is invited. Anyone can achieve it. Truth is only few believe it.

As we build and strengthen communities to make a difference, we'll want to use the power of learning to gain involvement. This involvement is a key ingredient in collaboration. If this is not understood, people could fear this type of change. As people become personally responsible, involved and engaged, we don't have to task people with activity. No one need parent or micromanage the participants. Instead the measure of success is dependent on the result the community produces. And again, results don't lie.

As we established earlier, change is inevitable. Don't fear change. It's proven that fear shuts down learning. We're wired that when we are in fear, we lose logic. Our brain is designed to shut down everything unimportant to survival—we're run by the fight or flight portion of our brain. Learning is key to creating solutions and being open to see new perspectives to navigate change which is inevitable.

The pilot who safely crash-landed an airliner on the Hudson River, Captain Sulley, commented that he just had to keep his emotions in check. He already knew exactly what to do with the plane and how to land to float it on the water because he had practiced it many times in the simulator. His learning had prepared him for that situation. Weird—yes! Coincidence—I don't think so. The only thing that could make his learning less effective was for him to become overwhelmed with fear and become paralyzed by his emotions—good reason to focus on physical and emotional wellbeing for our communities to succeed.

JOURNAL MOMENT

What learning are you focused on right now? Can you observe someone who's mastered what you are learning? Do you need to teach someone what you have learned? Are you fascinated by learning and do you learn from everywhere around you? What new things do you need to learn? Are you in fear right now? If so, identify that fear. Is it real? State the facts surrounding the situation. Now that you are aware of the fear and have listed the facts, can you see from a different perspective? Can you see a solution that you couldn't see before? Can you label the fear in a new way so it doesn't have power over you?

What can you learn from this? Who can help? Use learning to navigate change and keep fear from interfering with your fulfillment and future success.

The Value of Time And Money

What if you knew your job was ending today? Perhaps it's a career that you've invested many years in. What could be possible if you could replace your income? Or let's say you are getting behind on your mortgage and the interest rate is adjusting. Where are you going to turn to make some additional money? Will you take on a second or even third job just to keep things afloat?

Many people have to consider these questions and haven't had proper time to prepare. Financial freedom comes from simply making more money than you spend. It's not a difficult concept. It's simple but not as easy to execute with all of the commercialism demands of our world. You could constrain your spending to limit expenses to get there. Most think of the freedom of not having to focus daily on making an income or worrying about paying the bills. The goal is to transition from working hard for money to getting your money working for you. Examine how you make money and how you can keep more of the money that you make.

If you are always trading your finite time for dollars, you are making active income. With active income, if you are not putting in time, you aren't making money. If you're out sick or your kids are sick requiring you to stay home, you aren't making money because your time is not able to be used to make active income during these times. This is why it is hard to get ahead financially with just a job. It consumes your most precious resource – your time. Passive or residual income is money that comes in from an investment you've made that pays again and again. This income could be from real estate, businesses, royalties, commissions, or dividends. An example is that the work to make this book was done once and as long as they are distributed the royalties continue. The work was done once and the reward keeps coming. The same is true for one of my essential oil or nutritional supplement customers. They love the product and continue to order. I support them as they have questions but the work to teach them the value of wholesale customer membership was done and the rewards continue every time they choose to order. These types of income come in without demanding all of your time like an active income and the income continues long after your initial investment or activity.

Most people's financial troubles would be solved by just making more money. Many marriages would be saved with just a small amount of additional monthly income. Although this sounds simple, many aren't too creative to think of new ways to make more money. No, I'm not saying money fixes everything, or that the answer to all your problems is money. I'm saying if money is a source of stress in your life, finding a way to leverage your skills and make something happen will help. A money problem requires a money solution. There are so many opportunities around you right now. It doesn't matter whether the economy is good or bad. Opportunities always exist. The question really is, "Are you ready to do what it takes to make and attract more money?"

JOURNAL MOMENT

Answer this: "Are you ready to do what it takes to make more money?" And probably the most important question with regard to money is, "Are you open to receiving more money easily?" And, "Are you open to moving beyond your struggle with money?"

Are you willing to open your eyes to see the possibilities right now? Do you want to make more money now? Do you have time that you can invest in creating another source of income? Could you work full time on your job and part time or some time on your fortune?

What skills do you have that another could pay you for? What information do you know that you could create a product to teach others how to do something? Do you have an innovative product idea? Do you see a service that needs to be offered that people would pay for? Can you find a product that people want to buy and help expand the distribution? Are you already seeing a success with a local market that could easily expand nationally? How many ways can you think of that you could make money? What do people you know value? How can you help these people you know and meet get what they value? List them.

The Value of Business Ownership

Another key to success is to get money working for you instead of always working hard for money. This begins by gaining better tax advantages. Business owners have tax advantages allowing them to get more of their money working for them. Even if you work a job, if you start a business, you'll be able to take advantage from a tax perspective just by owning and operating that business. (And here's where you'll want to collaborate with a great tax professional!)

Since elementary school, we were taught to get a good education and get a job. It worked marvelously when there were jobs to be had, but now it's time to teach business ownership. You've seen kids make extra money by offering lawn mowing or babysitting services. Simply serving a need in the market is a great way to get a business started and to encourage budding entrepreneurs.

Have you investigated the power of the Internet to help you make money? My oldest when she was a teenager found out that if you get a following on YouTube with subscribers you can make money. So she built a web channel and focused her efforts on building her following. She'll have advertisers or contests, she'll make money doing what she loves and sharing it with the world.

The fascinating part about this option is that she figured this out all on her own. When I asked how she learned this, she told me she watched the way others were doing it. Modeling works and is the greatest of all teaching methods.

I'm seeing my youngest find things she is passionate about and she's developing videos to build a community online who is interested in her interests. Imagine if we engaged that inner creativity in more adults. What kind of a community could we create if we were supportive to new ideas instead of critical? Allow yourself to think freely here. Remove the limits. What if we listened with interest and thought of ways we could help each other succeed instead of staying quiet? What if we weren't so quick to quit on implementing our ideas? We've been taught to do our own work but we accelerate as we collaborate. As we share our wins and even what doesn't work, we strengthen our community to show a clear path toward success.

Did you know that you could start your own direct selling or network marketing business for as little as $50-$500? Many people are finding that making some extra income doesn't have to take a whole lot of time by offering valued products, ones that people want to buy, and being open to building a team of a few people who like to share the products with people they know and find who want them.

Maybe you have a technical ability allowing you to start a service business as I did for my first business in the mid 90's. I was a talented graphic designer working a corporate job. I began working part time picking up projects that I could work on in the evenings and weekends. Since I had great relationships with photographers, printers and advertising agencies, the projects found me. I worked this business part time for nearly a year while I still worked my corporate job that demanded over 40 hours a week. Then as it was easy for me to see that my part time business would sustain, I put all of my time and focus on making it fly. My decision was easy since I was making the same income in my side business as I was in my over full time demanding job. You can do the same if you have a talent or service that people want to buy. Again, it doesn't have to be hard. I attracted some crabs back then who pointed out that my new venture may fail as they asked what I would do if that happened. My answer was, "I guess I'll find another job." A simple answer and I got out of the corporate job bucket before they snagged me.

Or you could purchase a franchise where all of the systems needed in the business are figured out for you. Years ago I met Robert Needham who wrote *Wealth 3.0*. He had a passion for why we need to empower people to start their own businesses. In his case he encourages people to start a proven franchise to gain an initial advantage. Any business will give you a tax advantage. You'll be able to write off expenses and take advantage of laws beneficial for business owners. This will allow you to get more of your money working for you. Find something proven and put your efforts to expand it.

Some businesses will allow you to have flexibility of your schedule. This can be especially beneficial for families that have children or elderly parents to care for. With the help of technology, it's never been easier to operate your own business. This is just a door cracked open to the possibilities. If you do your research as the real you, pursuing what you really want, you could find a fruitful opportunity. Just seek it.

And know this—I love business! I'm interested in hearing your selection and I offer great questions to align the business with the lifestyle you desire. It's a hobby of mine now because I don't have to earn my livelihood from consulting anymore. So here's my reward for you making it here, two-thirds of the way through this book, on your way to being genuine and creating real value. Email me at nstrange@transformAnation.com to get help in selecting, aligning or expanding your business. Tell me your story so that I know where you are in the development process and your level of readiness to work and own your own business. I look forward to offering insight to assist your development.

I've taken countless people out for coffee as they got laid off from their jobs just to make sure they knew they were valuable (priceless and brilliant) before they went into any interviews. Remember Captain Sulley? He knew he could perform as long as he kept his emotions in check. Same is true here for suffering a loss of a job or career. Keep your emotions in check and remember your value. I've consulted hundreds of companies on improving marketing. And I've been a professional speaker offering over three decades of marketing expertise, and inspiring leadership development for the direct selling and network marketing industry for more than a decade. What I love the most is seeing people take action, share their vision, and seeing them progress on their path is so rewarding for me personally. I hope to hear from you.

  JOURNAL MOMENT

You can start a part time business right now. What type of business are you interested in? Why? What is your plan for switching from making active income to making more passive income? How can you take steps to create more money and get more of your money working for you? Are you ready to start on your way to financial freedom?

The Value of Self Confidence

Many people fear they just aren't cut out to sell anything. Some business owners hold themselves and their business back because of a sales phobia or insecurity. Most of these people have a negative mentality about selling.

Have you ever shared a product or service that you like with a friend? Do you remember how you spoke with excitement and conviction, and how they paid attention to you? Your energy attracted them. It was sincere. Your recommendation was strong. You were excited! This is selling and maybe you'd accept it easier if it was called influencing. When we find great value and have a good experience, it's easy to share our experience and influence another.

Promotion is something we do naturally. We want to share what works, what we believe in, what saves people time and money or what provides some benefit they want. You can learn to become more effective at communicating value and getting people to take action as you build more self-confidence. You can learn to ask for action and receiving money for the value you provide. First, you must build the belief and then receive the reward.

I am a person who believes I will find a great parking space. That might sound funny but I'm serious, I expect to find a parking place wherever I want it to appear and you know what? I do. My best friend used to believe he wouldn't find a parking spot near the door. He wouldn't even try and would beeline for the outskirts where there's always a spot. Guess who finds the great parking spot? I have no stress about parking and the years of modeling this are rubbing off! Much of that is set by what we focus on, what our intentions are, how we expect the world to show up and how our actions match our beliefs. Little or big, the way you see life directly affects it.

If you've been struggling for a while, you might not expect anything to change for you and your business. I totally understand. You've been working a long time and you aren't impressed with your personal results. You wonder whether it's worth trying any longer, and whether you're doing the right things to succeed eventually.

Just because someone else is successful doesn't mean that you can't be successful, too. There's room at the top for all of us if we are willing to do the inner work necessary to get there.

We are all a work in progress. Have you noticed the professional athletes who never stop improving their games, never stop hiring coaches and re-engineering their approach to maximize performance? In sports, you would expect to invest time practicing. You wouldn't expect to win without that commitment or sacrifice. If you want to improve your life or business results, it will take some action.

Olympic competitors practice their whole lives to prepare for one event. What commitment, diligence and follow-through to see it all the way to a win. It takes many wins to get into the games, let alone keep winning to the level of Olympic medals and breaking world records.

Where is your current belief about your chances for success? Consider just one new action you can take to move toward your goals and desires. One step, the next step, is the most critical for you to take action on to improve your situation. After that, it's just the next step that you need focus on.

JOURNAL MOMENT

Are you someone who is drawn to helping other people develop and become powerful? What is your belief about becoming successful? Do you prefer to lead or be a part of the organization? Why? List the type of work you enjoy and see how you can align this to your daily income-generating activities.

The Value of Relationships

Imagine a world that has been turned upside down. Unemployment is rising. Markets are uncertain. Now if this is all we had, I'd be worried. But I am not and let me share why.

Everything of value transfers through people. As Charlie "Tremendous" Jones offers, "You will be the same in 5 years except for the books you read and the people you meet." There is huge wealth in our connectedness and relationships. Empowerment comes through education, through the books we read. Our education or learning never stops. We can learn from everything around us.

Relationships are most important. And the good news is that people can be taught to build better relationships effectively and frequently. Your success will be multiplied as you build people up and serve others.

As you invest in developing your own effectiveness, you'll realize you can build belief and confidence to serve in any leadership capacity. The training and development I've attended and shared in my organization teaches people to be better communicators and become more capable leaders while we build our self-esteem and a positive self-image.

People have fragile places where things that have happened left scars. It changes the way they approach or don't approach opportunities. So if you feel vulnerable, afraid to approach someone to tell or sell something consider that scars might be contributing to that. I love mentoring people like you to help you gain effectiveness and see you overcome your fears of approaching people by learning to ask questions and serve others. You'd be amazed at how magnetically attractive you can become as we help you know yourself. Many of my friends call me a people weaver since I naturally connect people with synergy to meet and work with each other.

It can start simply with a real smile and direct eye contact. Send a silent message, "I'm glad to see you." Do you know how many people feel unloved and uncared for? Like no one wants to hear their thoughts and ideas. Do you feel this way? Some even try to be invisible. You might notice them as they keep their head down and walk briskly past you. In my own life I've seen people run out of church quickly to beat the crowd without saying anything to anyone. I notice them. Not because I think they're doing something wrong, but because I see they aren't connecting with others, which we all need. Make it your calling in life to notice opportunities like this, when you can reach out and connect like I do. You'll know it when you feel compelled to overflow into their lives.

There is so much to learn from each other every day. As you become excited to see people, learn to smile more, make eye contact and people will be attracted to you and wonder why you are so happy. They will see that you are unaffected by the doom and gloom of the current affairs or our negative media bombardment and they'll wonder why you have a different energy. This is the outward projection of your power and positive presence. When fulfillment is spilling over there's no room for the depleting negative stuff.

You could choose to accept and mirror the gloom and doom, perpetuating negative stories that circulate in our world. You can just as easily choose to look for the good in every situation, to be the bright spot in someone's day or to be an encouraging positive voice. Each of us has our gift to give someone else, yours may be different from mine, but connecting is the only way to make those gifts come alive.

Whatever your choice, you plant seeds. Select your seeds and await the harvest. After all, you don't plant an apple seed expecting an orange tree, right? Watch your thoughts, beliefs about others and spoken words about them carefully. How do you respond to negatives? Where do you see opportunities to connect? Learn to take correct action to build success. There will be no surprises come harvest time. Your results will be directly related to you doing the inner work and actively engaging in connecting and relating to others.

 JOURNAL MOMENT

What are you thinking, believing, and speaking right now? Notice what seeds you are planting. What can be done to serve your market? There is always another angle and a new approach to any situation. How can you serve?

HOW
DO YOU
MAKE A DIFFERENCE?

HOW DO YOU MAKE A DIFFERENCE?

Now that you are in action mode you know what fulfillment looks like, you know who overflowing impacts... Let's focus on the how. You are ready to see the actions and results to enhance your life and increase your own business. I believe in you, you won't hold yourself back anymore. You'll have clarity and focus.

I am all about creating a positive impact. Let's accomplish the best results while decreasing unnecessary effort along the way. This is when you show that you've shed your limiting thoughts, in actions that prove making a living doesn't have to be hard. If I do my job correctly, you'll invest less time and less money, grow faster and achieve higher returns on your investment. I'm so excited that you're ready for that. (You must be or you wouldn't be reading this right now.) Life is meant to flow effortlessly. Let's let it!

Do you know someone who accomplished a level of success only to find they couldn't sustain it? Have you seen someone go from company to company searching for "the magic company?" Let me tell you the truth right now. There is no magic company. There is no overnight sensation. Read success biographies and you'll see. People who are successful have become successful. They've prepared and built over their lifetimes. Many would have been successful no matter what because they had already answered what they really want. They planned and then took action to do what it took to fulfill the order. They saw opportunities for what they were and applied themselves fully. They were real with themselves and others about their pursuit.

You have tapped into owning your power, it's time for you to utilize it, time to test how effective you are. Some people have great skill to pull them forward and their success comes fast. It doesn't depend on time. Their success and their results depend on how effective they are, what opportunities they see and the action they take. They could quite frankly quit the company they are in and build from scratch, quickly achieving the same level of success in a brand new venture. They are successful not from what they do but from who they have become. That's fulfillment and it overflows naturally into others, and others, and more. So you achieving this will benefit many more than just you and your family.

It's been said that the most valuable six inches of real estate is between your ears. The knowledge that we gain and apply in our lives will achieve great success. The more effective we are at applying that knowledge, the faster we win.

People who seek out business success or financial books are eager to get busy and get into action. Just remember that aimless action will get you nowhere. People will follow your example. Leaders will want to be careful to match their words with their actions because what you do (or don't do) will be copied.

All effective leaders in direct sales or network marketing that I've talked with confirm that the keys to this business are consistency and persistency. Remember the marching cadence: "Left,

left, left, right, left"? Here's a new one for you: "Consistency, Persistency! Consistency, Persistency!" Try marching to that. At your tough breakthrough times, (and believe me, you will have them), simply repeating these two words with each step left and right, can help you keep taking another step. Many who are speaking from the stages at conventions will confess that their secret to success was just not quitting. This is what forces you into reality, when something is consistent it gains credibility, when it persists through the tough times it gains dependability. It's solid. It's real. That's important.

How Can I Serve You?

The best words I ever learned. Thanks McDonalds! Yes, I clocked some hours at Mickey D's. They taught me to look people in the eye, smile and ask, "How can I help you?" Though, I found the word "serve" has more depth, it's the same idea. These actions and words have served me well over the years. They can serve you well too. Asking how to serve someone, what they need, is far more powerful than pushing your agenda on them and trying to sell them something.

My daughter works at Starbucks and I've seen firsthand how their training program teaches their employees to connect. You may not have noticed it but as you are sharing your individual name and nuances of your drink request, they are skilled at engaging in conversation with you. How validated a well-placed, open-ended question can make you feel. This is a skill that anyone can learn; even the most introverted of personality types.

I travel extensively teaching groups and individuals how to become more effective at business and how to remove barriers to what they really want. I begin my workshops and leadership seminars by first honoring the participant's investment of time. Then, I ask them that important question, "How can I serve you?" You see even though people paid to attend the workshop, their time was the most precious investment. They could always make more money, but they could never replace the time that they invested in being mentored for the day. So giving the power to direct our day of mentoring allows them to gain exactly what they came to my training for—everyone wants to be seen and heard. Then it's easy to teach them skills that work with their personality and opportunity. This was divinely revealed to me. People just need to be seen and heard. Notice I didn't say want… they really do need it.

Think about your journey through this book. Now that you see yourself and your time and effort differently, it's time to rise to occasion. You are now someone that others can resource. If you will look at the people that cross your path every day with compassion and simply see them and hear them, you will increase your leadership power and abilities substantially. I dare you to try it. Lead with your heart, be present, and sincerely see and hear people. I think you'll be amazed at how effective this is. And, it feels great! It's the win/win we talked about.

First, they will feel true connection that they may not have felt in a long time. They're not invisible anymore as you notice them. Smiles are exchanged. Even on this level it's profound to see what happens when humanity connects. Then, as you have opportunity, ask them a question and listen. Allow them to express themselves without you having an agenda. This allows them to be heard. No judgment. You certainly don't need to debate either. They will feel a caring concern from you that may be foreign or even strange to them. But they will feel you heard them. Be sincere. Don't manipulate.

Try this and let me know what you discover. I really want to hear from you. You'll learn what other people really want. You'll gain understanding of different perspectives adding to your overall wisdom of people. You'll learn to listen and really hear people. I wouldn't be surprised if you see natural connections that may help them but save that for another future conversation or follow up. For now, just get good at relating and connecting. It seems to be a lost art.

Another revealing question is, "What do you want to learn more about so you can get better results?" It may be that you don't own a business but want to. Take this process and my suggestions to any area of your life and adapt it to fit your needs. This isn't about me telling you anything. The goal is to help you discover what you need to focus on to realize your purpose in life. The first step is to plant the question and let you feel safe in asking this question for your own progress.

As you begin to let life flow effortlessly and make a difference to create real value, plan to be a great leader.

Overflow & Encouraging Others

Now that you're claiming your power and getting a taste of what that looks like, there may be times when you find yourself in the role of counselor or mentor. Especially as you develop yourself past fulfillment and begin to actively overflow. Others will come to you for guidance and they'll need your leadership. Notice that people you attract will probably be working on some of the same issues you have worked on. First understand that there is a tender human being in your presence. Treat them with gentleness and kindness since you don't know where they've been and what they are dealing with in their lives at that moment. Never assume anything! Lead them to become aware of what's possible around them. Ask questions to guide them to own their development. Be careful not to tell or push them. Instead, by asking questions and sharing your own experiences, you compel them to take responsibility for their development. Help them discover how to release fear. Since you are still on your own journey, this may sound exhausting, but don't worry. That's the beauty of fulfillment. You're full to the brim and overflowing, so serving and encouraging others won't deplete you.

Some people relinquish control of their lives over to others. Some will find a way to turn it to serve their negative needs, confirming that they are exactly what they think they are—victims. If this is something that you have experienced in your life, either now or in the past, make the choice to take back control. Only you can decide to make this shift. It may not be easy, but it is possible. The difference this will make will not only affect your life but the lives of those around you. Remember, you liberate others as you shine brightly!

Some say this is just personal responsibility or accountability, but I believe a business-owner mindset is more than that. It comes from a knowingness of who genuinely I am combined with a selfless care for others. It's expressed in a servant leadership style and seen in being present to listen, understand and solve issues considering all parties involved. Perhaps it's more closely aligned with diplomacy.

As your business structures shift and economies ebb and flow, we need to better understand communities and collaboration. Greed will not win out. Quantity will not replace quality. People seek value. Value is more than money. It's relationships that are the key to our success.

Corporate organizations will need to shift their focus on reframing their environments. The behaviors of the past that have been so deeply engrained into the corporate culture will not contribute to the twenty-first century business success. Leading organizations will and are already investing into their people development in a different way. Entrepreneurs like myself will lead in teaching culture adjustment sharing the strengths we've developed. Equipped with new knowledge, value creation leaders will empower their organizations to collaborate, connect and create real value while adopting a community culture.

Each day, I personally set out to do two things:

❏ Build quality relationships
❏ Create value in my community

Remember our starting thoughts: "If you had all of your time and more than enough money, who would you be? What would you do? What would you like to have?"

Focus on building quality relationships every day. Resources flow through relationships. Money and opportunity are resources that you need to attract and manage to become successful. Relationships form community. Everyone plays a part in building the community. Collaboration is key to accelerating results for everyone. It's the power of our Collective Intelligence and it is the answer to transforming our world.

My focus is to create value in my community every day. A community could be defined as a family, neighborhood, organization, department, team, customers, niche groups or an entire market. The value I bring impacts the whole economy. This creates a positive ripple effect. As we band together to build our communities, we will strengthen our economy. We cannot overlook local for global. It takes both to make a strong world economy.

Understand that as a leader or mentor, people will watch you more intently. As a parent, I learned this early on and am continually reminded of how we are observed. One of my daughters made comment when she was a toddler as we were running a little late one day, "Mommy, are you going off speed limit?" They notice everything! When it finally came time to get her driver's permit, I utilized every car trip as a live example. Even then, I found myself defending my seasoned driver habits, "Don't do this. I have many years of driving experience!"

Don't let this shake you, no one expects you to be perfect as a leader. As you strive to be your best, you'll need to rise to the occasion. Matching your talk and walk is crucial. It's not about trying to be perfect, perfect isn't real. Being real is what this is all about. You'll begin to realize that many things can erode your progress. If you want to be most efficient, decide ahead of time how you want to be and then keep your actions in line with your focus and purpose. For instance, if you like things to happen efficiently, then don't show up late or miss deadlines. You are in charge of you. You create your existence. Your attention to these details will accelerate or slow your progress. Now you know you can choose how you want to move along the journey. These actions are the practice of your belief. They only deepen with time, becoming more and more a part of your fabric.

When you mentor or lead people, see if there is one action that they can do to shift the pattern. Love them just the way they are and help them set one goal they can achieve. Think baby steps, but in a sequence where they can cover a lot of ground and experience progress. Then help them set another goal. As you empower them to take a step ahead, they will be rewriting their future breaking the bondage of their past. Ultimately, it's up to them to choose to participate. Your role is to encourage them to become aware and help them identify what steps they can take.

I will caution you: don't take on another's burden. We all have to make it to the top on our own. You can choose to lighten the load or unconsciously drag everything up the mountain with you. I have a mentor who teaches the suitcase principle. It goes like this: Imagine as someone shares details of their situation that it's their dirty laundry being shared with you as if they've opened up a suitcase. They pull out different items complaining or explaining why they are stuck at any point in their development. As they go on and on, let them be the ones with the suitcase and the items they are showing. As the conversation ends, see the suitcase closing with all of their items tucked back inside. Then as they leave your presence, imagine them taking the entire suitcase with them. This visualization and principle has allowed me to be involved and impactful in many people's situations while staying free. It protects me from taking their suitcase and piling the burden on my back with my own. I can certainly add value and comment or share expertise or give them considerations but I cannot—I will not—carry their burden.

 JOURNAL MOMENT

Identify if you are playing the part of a victim in any area of your life. If so, how can you set boundaries to take back your power? Write the victim behavior so you can plan an alternate action or attitude that puts you back in your personal power. You teach people how to treat you. If you don't respect yourself, how do you expect others to respect you? It starts with the commitment you make to yourself. As you decide you are ready to change patterns, you can plan how you'll take positive action in these situations that used to leave you defeated. Are there people in your life right now that are looking to you for leadership? If you find that they are behaving from a weakened victim perspective, engage in a discovery conversation to see if they are ready and willing to change the pattern. If so, run them through the process of answering the questions in this book. Make sure to have them write out their answers. They are to take action to change their own patterns. You are merely a guide. Your role is to facilitate them taking action and suggesting or questioning them to help the discovery process.

PASS-I-ON

Another way you'll lead people is by inspiring them. Passion is unbeatable. It's contagious. Magnetic. Align your passion with your action and focus and you are sure to find success. Passion is the final ingredient of fulfillment. You will be inspired from the inside not needing to be pushed or motivated externally.

Have you ever looked at the word Passion? I often find clues inside of words. Passion is how I Pass-I-On, which to me means it's how I share what I really care about on to another person. Recently, I realized that passion can be anger against something just as much as love for something. Both create fuel and spark action and momentum. One is fueled by moving away from something they don't want to tolerate anymore; the other is fueled by going for what they want intensely and experience more of it.

Let your passion be discovered and be careful of only sharing and not listening. This can be hard when you're excited about something. I saw uncontrolled passion harm independent distributors in direct selling and network marketing. These new distributors would get so emotionally excited about their product or business opportunity that they completely shut down as a receptive human being. They transformed into a passionate and unstable flame thrower, scorching every contact that crossed their path. They excitedly dumped on those around them and pushed people away. Repelling instead of attracting. Imagine a flame thrower setting a field of dry grass on fire. One time coming too close to the flame and you'll remember to stay clear of those wild glazed eyes forever.

Instead, let your passion gently overflow. If people are thirsty, they will find the cup that overflows and take part. When you overflow, those who are looking for your products, services or business opportunity will come to you. Listen with all senses with the 4:1 ratio in mind: two eyes, two ears to one mouth. It's refreshing when someone really listens and can share something of significance. As people speak, they reveal what they are dissatisfied with and what pains or discomforts they have. As a business owner, I can choose to solve these subtle requests or make introductions to people who can solve these issues. When you can connect with someone on a deeper level, you can have a real and more meaningful exchange and that forms a lasting impression. As I invite others who want my leadership to come up and fill their cup from mine, we can bring life to the room, the community, city, state, country, and world. This is the example of effectively passing along passion. It's how I pass myself on to lead others. It's how I inspire action in others who are ready to take action.

Fulfill Up – Real Collaboration

It's not just about giving, leading and inspiring. You will find leadership, inspiration and resources too. I mentioned the Collective Intelligence, think of it as your bank of wisdom. I know it's possible to make a big difference, but it requires your participation. I've known for a long time after watching the Pixar animated film, *A Bug's Life*, that if we ants get together and help one another, we can overcome any "grasshopper" problem or challenge.

Relationships will be the key to your success. Identifying people that you want to learn from, grow with and who challenge you to rise to a better you are the kind of people attracted to our community. Technology allows us to interconnect but nothing replaces the physical interaction and relationship development that takes place at a live event. The positive environment that is created when like-minded people get together in a collaborative way is priceless. I find I learn so much more than just the content delivered in these types of environments. That's the power of Collective Intelligence.

Remember, negative headlines can't take down the spirit of entrepreneurism in our country. As we work together to support each other we can all reach success beyond our expectations. Coming together sparks a better conversation. Peer to peer support is powerful as we encourage and enlighten each other to take action. We share experiences and learn from each other what works and what doesn't. Creative thinking can solve our problems. You can easily create an extra income stream or formulate a business launch to be more successful as you work together with us.

We've seen a shift from offline to online and now that pendulum is swinging back. This will create a great advancement in technology that supports relationship development. There is something special about the power of a group that works together. They are more impactful than a mass that has no knowledge of one another. Our cause is to support this type of group allowing the organization to grow organically but purposefully. We are here to help more people like you become successful faster and sustainably.

Success doesn't come without setbacks or bumps. I remember watching some children as they worked to perfect skateboard tricks at a local park. Their persistence was amazing. They would keep attempting again and again a particular move. They would fall, get up and try again. Never did they sit out and give up. Never did they imagine that one attempt was enough. They embodied the principle of fail forward faster. They all supported one another with encouragement and they celebrated as the trick was performed to satisfaction. Imagine the difference if the person completed the trick with no one watching. Yes, there would be a sense of accomplishment but all the sweeter when there was a support network to cheer them on.

As adults we hold on too tight sometimes. Our image and pride is wrapped up in a persona we are selling and we want to have control over it. This puts us in critical seats, acting as a judge and not allowing us to expand with the necessary bumps and stretches that come our way. This judgment is dominating many people's perspectives right now. They may be determining their self-worth by the balance or lack of money, in their bank account. They may now feel useless as they retire from a life-long career. They may have just had the rug ripped out from under them as they suffered a job loss or business failure due to the current economic constraints. The negativity accompanying this judgment is poison and it shuts down our creative ability to think of new solutions or see opportunity. It encourages quitting or giving up on our divine purpose. As we come together in a community, your role is to encourage others, share resources and contacts to help each other now more than ever. People need to be reminded that they are priceless!

We win when we go forward faster, making more than enough money to take care of our needs and build the lifestyle we want. When? Now. Win now! Then we have the means to invest in areas aligned with our purpose. We are able to teach others to follow our example. You've done great work through this book. You've begun to follow this process to improve your personal and business results.

You've already begun to prepare for the journey to your success. Now I've shared with you why I want you to join us and take action. I've invited you to be a part and create what's possible first for yourself and your family, and then for your friends and community. Let's lead our lives to make a difference and create real value in our communities. It's just like on the airplane. We have to put on our own oxygen mask first. Then we can help our neighbor.

 JOURNAL MOMENT

And yes, here's an opportune journaling moment. What I'd really love is for you to share your story with me at nstrange@ transformAnation.com. Together, I do believe we can truly transform-a-nation. I think we can build a better world! I would love for you to add your voice and be encouraged by the experience of others as I build out a community of support. Share how you've taken action with the learning shared here and how that has positively impacted your life or business. Tell me how you are being genuine and making a difference. Share the value you are creating. Draw attention to the value we need to create and let the Collective Intelligence of like-minded people to come together to produce results.

I care about you and your success!

Attract Opportunities

Dr. John Dewey said that one of the greatest desires people have is the "desire to be great." We feel it when we're ready to quit playing small. Does that sound like you right now? As you develop your awareness and ask better questions, you draw answers. People show up in your life to introduce you to your next steps. It doesn't stop with this process, this process is the beginning.

I made a decision to not play small and developed into a leader helping people gain more impact in their life or business. It was over a decade of development and I'm sure I'm not done yet. In fact I don't believe there's such a thing as "done" when it comes to greatness. I'm committed to being a life-long learner. I learn from everything. As I reflected on my path of development, I discovered value that was created from different segments. At the time I hadn't seen that these segments fit together but looking back each gave me a significant part. I'm sharing my experience because that is what I know. That's what I have to give you. You have your own experience that may be totally different, so learning the ideas is the focus here. What can you learn from your experience to see if you are headed in the best direction? I've seen clues that may help guide you so think about these as you read and then you can journal more as we take a walk through my past.

First, I invested in my own development with time and money. I attended many seminars and events to learn the steps to become a better business owner, more impactful speaker and how to inspire more people to gain success. I attracted great mentors and strategic partners whose relationships are critical to helping me on my path. The connections I developed built a support group of like-minded people around me. No one goes alone.

It's practice time—are you connecting with people who can help you on your path? I leveraged other people's experiences to expand my knowledge. That created short cuts in my path. Having relationships with people ten, twenty and even thirty years older than me has been life-changing. I can learn from their experiences and hear their wisdom to consider as I progress along my success path.

My knowledge grew due to broadening my perspective. I began to work with more speakers and authors helping them develop their brand and products. I learned more about building a successful information business by studying different leaders in this field and attending varied seminars. I saw the power of automation, collective systems and internet marketing. I participated in helping concept a new conference center business model increasing my passion to help people with personal development and learn leadership skills. I spent years training and developing effective leaders in direct selling and network marketing helping them become better business owners. Delivering transformational leadership events, I witnessed people gaining their own life-changing results. All of this time, I was strengthening my own personal development into becoming an impact-ful, compassionate leader.

Your own knowledge and experience become assets too. Changing your perspective opens new thoughts, doors and experience. Are you gaining the necessary knowledge and experience needed for your success? Do you need a change of perspective to add to your development or get you out of a rut?

For me, open doors came in the form of invitations to the faculty of business organizations that taught entrepreneurs how to launch and accelerate their businesses. My speaking invitations increased as people learned that my guidance got results. Even though there are many people that share similar knowledge, participants of my events or mentorship would comment how they felt empowered and were inspired to act on the knowledge I shared. I discovered I have a gift for taking a vast amount of information drilling it down into simple, actionable steps. I didn't realize that I spoke in a way that allowed these same concepts taught by others to be quickly understood and actionable.

Take an assessment of your unique gifts. Too many times these go unnoticed and unharnessed. Listen to what others speak about as your strengths, embracing compliments fully will give you skill highlights. Are you leveraging these strengths in your actions?

I listened to the concerns and personal blocks my audiences had and it seemed what they needed most was to be aware of what was stopping them and how to take a simple action in the right direction. When I asked the audience, "How can I serve you?", and shared exactly what they wanted to learn, not necessarily what I had prepared ahead of time to speak about, they felt more served than ever before. The learning was relevant and real, the best way to honor them and their time. This developed a rapid loyalty and deep connection. Trust was established quickly because they knew I heard them. They were understood, so they understood me and the wisdom I shared.

Members of these audiences commented that they had made life-changing decisions using the three steps we went over in this book. Some even applied the newly gained knowledge to their family life. Leaders were developed and found themselves to be more effective. Business owners gained a clearer understanding of marketing and branding and learned how to increase their sales. The key that I found was to create awareness, teach what was relevant and facilitate the audience to take responsibility to take action with the material immediately. As leaders, we inspire action. And without action, nothing changes.

It's important to listen to your market as you pursue what you really want and find fulfillment. This will help you move toward a career that is in demand or guide you to build a business that has real potential. One of the first pieces of advice I give to businesses I consult is to have them listen to their existing market. This includes asking previous customers or clients what they want and need to see if the offerings of the business need adjustment. At its most basic, this is just good old market feedback. I'm amazed at how many business owners who have not learned the power of asking questions and listening. It seems many have gotten into the telling and selling mode trying too hard to convince people that they've forgotten this valuable principle of business. They think they have to know it all. It's true that no one cares how much you know until they first know how much you care.

Your business exists to solve your customer's problem by answering their question, "how can you serve me?" every single day. As you serve that customer, you get the opportunity to develop a life-long relationship for as long as they see value in your business. This value is in the relationship not the transaction. It's not about what you make that's important. It's about what you make possible for your customer.

Now more than ever, it is important for people to make money and get results faster. There is more competition for the same job these days. Consumers want more value from the businesses they frequent. I'm always sharing how to distinguish yourself or your business from the competition. It's a key component you'll want to build if you want to accelerate your success. This works whether you own your business or if you are an employee. There's always a way to better connect and relate to build your value. With so much information, it is so easy to fall into mediocrity and lose your voice. Standing out is possible and critical for you to get your message where it needs to go. This is the beginning of your influence and real value.

It's much easier to become a leader when you magnetically attract people to want to follow you. People need to learn to become better connectors and develop stronger relationships. Businesses can't afford missing opportunities due to people not representing the brand correctly. Marketing that magnetizes your prime customer is much more effective than marketing that yells to everyone around you. It takes focus and planning to become magnetic – both personally and in your marketing. You'll want to choose wisely to build your personal brand and your business brand.

Your personal brand or business brand is very valuable. Since you never get a second chance to make a first impression, it's critical to develop in the areas that give you the most impact. If you're working a job, your presence is being evaluated the whole time. If you own a business, people are choosing to do business with you first and your business second. You may have heard the phrase, "People do business with people they know, like and trust." So your presence, your first impression, is something to pay attention to increase your results. It might just be the area that is holding you back from getting the positive impact you desire.

I teach people to have a powerful presence, to attract more to them with less effort and to achieve results faster. It only takes seconds to decide whether you trust someone, want to do business with them, believe them or want to be involved with them. One key is to be yourself—be real—people can spot a fake.

People are tired of hype, empty promises and busy work. No one wants to be sold but everyone wants to find something of real value. Especially if this real value satisfies a need they have. People will invest in things that produce real results all the time. And, they will share what works with many of their contacts providing a continual stream of introductions and referrals. So as you invest in relationships, the return comes in continuing referrals and an unlimited supply of business opportunity.

 JOURNAL MOMENT

Keep your ears open to discover opportunities. What value can you bring to people you know? What opportunities are you seeing that you could focus on? What have you noticed by listening to the people you serve? If you have been in business for a while, when is the last time that you asked your past customers how you might better serve them? Are there people who don't know what you are up to who might be able to open doors if you'd share your vision?

How do you rank against the competition? How could you deliver more value? What improvements could you make to your personal presence or business service? How are the people that work for you or your business at connecting with people? Are you missing opportunities? What comes to mind to add value to your personal presence or business brand? How well do you relate and connect with people? What could it mean if you were a better at networking?

This Isn't The End!

A journey begins with the next step. Once you've established the direction you'll head and the destination so you'll know when you reach it, there's only one thing left to do. Take the next step. Focus and refocus only on this question, "What *is* the next step?" This will keep you moving ahead and keep you from getting overwhelmed by all the things you don't know or can't see yet.

If you're an action person like me, maybe you sat through the end of that powerful movie, *Pay It Forward*, feeling the spirit of involvement, freshly inspired, ready to go and then felt shock as the movie ended and the screen went black—without a call to action. I couldn't get over the lost opportunity to champion a ton of actions. I need a hefty "Go do this! Go do that!" Certainly, many viewers did pick up and go do something, but the movie could have transformed things with their captive audience right then and there.

If you only read this book, you'll only retain about 10% it. Responding in your journal helps it stick more. Answer the questions and think about them as they become more relevant to your life. Add to them and share what you've added with your community. Discuss this material and share experiences that exemplify the concepts. Blog about this and teach it to others. The best way to learn is to experience the whole process. Imagine what a difference you'll make as you let your life flow effortlessly and create real value with us everywhere at every age!

Let us know how we can support you. What do you need? How can I serve you? Ask about support for your group, organization, association or company with a variety of customizable solutions. Can I benefit your efforts by scheduling a presentation or a conference call for you and your organization?

Stephen R. Covey says, "Begin with the end in mind." Your beginning is our end goal. Your success. What a thrill it is to receive your comments and e-mails about how you've applied this process, improved your impact and gotten results—in your businesses, and also in your personal lives. Please keep us updated and share how you've applied this to your life and how it is now flowing much more effortlessly than before you believed, decided and acted on being the best you that you could be. Email me your thoughts, invite me to speak with your team, your group, your business. Join the Collective Intelligence, we want you to be in the conversation nstrange@transformAnation.com

You are an amazing human being with no limits! Remember, fulfillment is simple and it's your belief, decision and action that makes what you really want—your success—possible. Let's pledge to embrace LIFE Let It Flow Effortlessly and take action to be genuine and create real value. We can build better communities with great and powerful servant leaders like you.

Lifeometer

 JOURNAL MOMENT

Let's check in. It has been some time since you opened your eyes to a new way of living life. And you may have found yourself picking up and putting down this book. Since LIFE is a journey not a destination, it benefits you to revisit some of the questions from earlier sections. Here are questions you've already been asked, but you'll find here as you answer them now, your answers might have changed or become more refined, because you've changed. Remember the balloon? Take a moment to reflect and answer these questions again now in this present moment. Revisit this list regularly and note what's changed. Your development can be seen as you reflect on your different journal entries.

- ❏ What crabs do you hear and what are they saying that might limit your success?
- ❏ Are they afraid they won't fit into your new life if you succeed?
- ❏ Are the words you use empowering or diminishing?
- ❏ What direction do you want to steer your life?
- ❏ Are you steering at all right now?
- ❏ Would you treat any friends or acquaintances the way you treat yourself? Would they still be your friend if you did?
- ❏ How are you?
- ❏ How do you feel?
- ❏ What is your powerful affirmation?
- ❏ What do you think about money?
- ❏ What do you think about success?
- ❏ How do you see yourself?

❑ How would you introduce your genuine self?

❑ Why is this your focus?

❑ Is now the right time for you?

❑ What do you want to remember about what you've just read and how it applies to you now?

❑ When have you accomplished something that challenged your fears and previous limits?

❑ What do you want?

❑ What will you do?

❑ What's possible now?

After you've answered these again, make note on what surprises you've discovered. Check in and feel your body and what living your purpose feels like. Just knowing you exist and are capable of great things shifts your health and wellbeing. This is why I'm all in focusing on empowering people to improve their circulation and cellular health. As we get this going in the right direction, we can improve physical and emotional wellbeing. And great leaders need their full wellbeing to operate at the highest level of performance.

SHARING HOPE -
HELPING OTHER PEOPLE
EVERYDAY, EVERYWHERE
AND IN EVERY WAY

SHARING HOPE - HELPING OTHER PEOPLE EVERYDAY, EVERYWHERE AND IN EVERY WAY

EXTRA: What I Personally Know Is Possible

I love words and the clues I find within them. You may have seen it written as "Impossible" and then as an apostrophe is added it becomes "I'm possible." I've utilized this in my speaking as I write my name "Norma S. Strange" and add an apostrophe to change it to "Norma's Strange." Embrace your own unique design. Here's some things that I know are possible in my life that may help expand your creative thinking to unlock potential for you if you're willing to open your eyes and mind to become success now. Let's play!

It's possible...

- ❑ To accelerate business success through effective training and mentoring.
- ❑ To be born on Christmas day and not feel cheated by getting half birthday/half Christmas presents. My mom told me I was the best Christmas present she ever received.
- ❑ To be tall and not play basketball or volleyball.
- ❑ To not be a waitress the rest of my life just because I majored in commercial art and graphic design.

- ❑ To be named Strange and act pretty normal.
- ❑ To be a successful mom working as an entrepreneur and not sacrifice my family for my professional success.
- ❑ To have choice to receive all that is possible.
- ❑ To solve the world's problems by collaborating, combining our talents, and creating unlimited solutions.
- ❑ To learn to dive in the deep end of the pool at two years old and swim like a fish.
- ❑ To ride a unicycle up and down steep hills in the Virginia mountains.
- ❑ To be utterly speechless as you see your children born and grow up to be wonderful loving hearts sharing their uniqueness with the world.
- ❑ To walk on stilts through mud puddles without falling down.
- ❑ To choose to love myself and others unconditionally, and feel better about myself in the process.
- ❑ To stop judgment just like a cancer and rid it from my relationships.
- ❑ To hear, see, and communicate even if you're blind, deaf and mute. I celebrate the wisdom of Helen Keller and what a legacy she left us.
- ❑ To show us the world from a different perspective and have us laugh out loud. Thank you Gary Larsen.
- ❑ To learn good money principles, like Warren Buffet's two rules of money: #1 Don't lose any money. #2 Never forget rule number one.
- ❑ To learn from experience—our own and others'--and pass that on. I've had the privilege of knowing many mentors and wise folks who were 10, 20, and 30 years older than I. Their wisdom helped me go farther, faster.

❑ To not speak to someone for years but know that our hearts still care for one another even though much time has passed by.

❑ To reconnect after decades of time has passed and pick up friendship right where we left off.

❑ To forgive and forget if I am willing to release anger and pride.

❑ To work in business partnership and make it a success.

❑ To listen with a 4:1 ratio – two eyes, two ears to one mouth. Or perhaps even more accurate, 7:1 ratio – two eyes, two ears, one empathic heart, one knowing gut, one infinite intuitive spirit to one mouth.

❑ To hear and understand another's perspective without having to sacrifice my own beliefs and values.

❑ To agree to disagree but to love and honor each perspective.

❑ To change the world with a thought put to action.

❑ To build a training center where people come from all over the world to build themselves: first as a person, then for the business idea they want to venture.

❑ To teach entrepreneurs arming them with principles and wisdom that supports them to make decisions at the pace of business.

❑ To deliver value and create win-wins.

❑ To collaborate more and accelerate wins.

❑ To share my heart without fear.

❑ To look people in the eye and be present with them and celebrate the gift of a present moment.

❑ To be fully present for the gift of today and not worry at all about things far away—past or future.

❑ To replace fear with love; it wins out every time.

❑ To watch for opportunities to open a door or give someone a hug.

- ❑ To feed a man for a lifetime, teach him to lead others teaching them to fish.
- ❑ To silently pray to my God, to pray for anyone no matter what their belief, to live compassion for each living creature.
- ❑ To share this message with you. I hope you'll do the same and share the difference you're making with me at nstrange@transformAnation.com. I'd love to hear your story. You matter to me!

Words To Live By

"...You shall love the Lord your God with all your heart, and with all your soul, and with all your mind. ...You shall love your neighbor as yourself."

(New American Standard Bible, Matthew 22.37-39)

There is no other piece of wisdom more impactful to my success as learning and living these words each and every day. As you are filled with love from God, you learn to love yourself and this then fills you up and spills over to love others unconditionally. Self-acceptance gives us great strength and confidence to be inspiring leaders. When we connect and collaborate, we strengthen our communities, build better businesses and invent new solutions. I am optimistic of our future as we combine our Collective Intelligence to reach unlimited potential.

Choose BLISS

I've shared my thoughts and experiences with you in hopes that it will create for you BLISS. This is an acronym that was divinely inspired as I decided to quit being a human doing and becoming a human being. Here's what the BLISS principle of success is:

B = Believe

For me this means to believe in God the Father, the Son and the Holy Spirit. For some you may take this to mean to believe that you have a unique purpose, have a dream, and were created to fulfill that success. I recommend reading Bruce Wilkinson's *The Dream Giver* to help support the exploration of following your dream. I've found this book to be very encouraging as I step out in faith and walk the path God has created for me. For some others it may simply mean to believe in yourself or your dream as having the potential for success. You were created with a specific purpose in life and one that is unique to you and you only. What a shame it would be if the world missed out on it if you did not believe that you could realize it. You have not been created to fail. If God brings you to it, He'll get you through it and this means He'll provide you the strength to carry it forward. Believe in yourself, your talents and your purpose. For more encouragement on this, Rick Warren's *The Purpose Driven Life* book is a wonderful study.

L = Let Go

This is the humbling part of the success principle. For me it is clear to let go and let God. This means to let go of the past and any failures that you may have. Let the past pass by and remain. You cannot hold onto the flood of success that God has for you just as you cannot hold in your hands a river flowing. Let go of circumstances. Let go of how it will happen and be open to receive it the way it is planned. Let go grows faith. Let go humbles and removes our pride. Our success is not about us as much as it is about God giving it to us.

I = Inspired

Once you believe and let go, you will be fully inspired as only God can do. This will increase your creativity and inspiration. You will be more productive than ever before. You won't have those limiting beliefs that the world places on you. You will become more of who God created you to be. You'll attract to you whatever it is that you need to succeed. Inspiration is something that flows to me as I'm moving in my divine direction. Think of the simple directions of this word—LIVE. In one direction it's vibrant and exciting as we live our diving purpose. Flip the word and look at the other direction—EVIL. You'll know the results you'll get just by seeing the direction you're pointed. Keep your eyes on your divine purpose. You were made to manifest the glory of God.

S = Slow Down

This is where today's world misses the boat completely. All worldly wisdom points to doing more, longer hours and more effort. This actually pushes things away from us. Going faster causes more stress which is becoming a top health concern contributing to many diseases. Slowing down allows us to be fully present in our relationships. It allows for better connection within our community. It allows us to gain necessary wisdom. Slowing down allows us to get done what is most important and leave the rest to tomorrow to sort out. We fall victim to multiple voicemail boxes, emails, texts, messages, correspondence and meetings. If we follow in the way of the world, we are doomed to nonproductive activities that leave us exhausted, distracted, and empty. My friend shares a caution about being busy. She shared that BUSY means being under Satan's yoke. No matter your belief, think of how distractions rob us of being present. Think of how we don't connect well when we are busy. Just notice how much you are busy and know it robs you of the gift of being present. Pay attention to what's making you busy. Be focused. Be active, but watch out for being busy or being in busy-ness instead of being in your business on purpose. God knows what is best for us and gives us his peace. This peace is a peace that passes all human understanding. It is refreshing. It comes easiest from slowing down, being in study of the Word and asking him in prayerful dialogue what is most important today. It is how this book got written down. Because God wanted it done. There were other demands for my time but I've been listening and I felt that he was telling me it was time to share this message with you. There is no accident that you are reading this right now.

S = Succeed

Believe. Let Go. Inspiration overflows. Slow Down. Succeed. This is the new formula for success. It is not for the weak in Spirit. It is for those who are chosen, those who have been adopted as children of God, fellow members of the body of Christ. You are already a success. How can you arrange your life to unencumber yourself from the distractions and disappointments of the current moment to hear your call? What is God asking you to do? Where are you to put your efforts?

If you are looking for answers, talk with someone you trust and you may just find yourself saying the answer to them. Find a good mentor or listening partner and meet regularly to help each other. Form a mastermind with a small group of people that want to experience collective wisdom. Embrace our community invitation here and let's create a space where you can let your life flow effortlessly and connect with like-minded people who want to make a difference, leave a legacy and create real value in this world.

Three LIFE Changing Minutes

I couldn't catch my breath. I'd been feeling pressure in my chest as I drove into work that hot Arizona morning. It wasn't the extreme dry heat that caused this. As I entered the office building I was greeted with the bad news—air conditioning was out in the offices. My boss suggested that we move our work over to the companion company that he also headed up. I knew this was a bad idea for me this particular day. I could feel my heart beat increasing faster and faster as I struggled to let breathing just happen. I knew it was no coincidence that I was seeing constraint and no breathing room, no life anywhere around me. I could almost hear the ambulance sirens again. I'd been here before more than a decade earlier. But what was different then was I knew that lack of sleep for three days with lots of caffeine, the fuel for the deadline back then, was responsible for sending me into a full body panic. This time I didn't realize that sustained stress over time can be a sneaky killer, and the number one enemy of effortlessness in your life.

I was lucky enough to have essential oils in my home when I hit this wall of overwhelming stressful feelings, a build-up of over three years. I felt like something was awfully wrong. I had made it home using the broken air conditioner and not feeling well to get me out of that office building for the day. I wasn't sure that I might just have to call for medical assistance. It was a last ditch to try something in the comfort of my home to see if I might get some relief. I grabbed my essential oils and prayed they would work.

I am always pleased to share my testimony and how I felt called to start building a doTERRA essential oil business to serve customers, empower leaders, and educate a healer in every home worldwide. The company formed in 2008 with a vision of providing essential oil integrity that didn't exist in the industry. Their vision—empower families with essential oils in every home with doTERRA—the name means "gift of the earth." I received that gift!

I used doTERRA's Balance grounding blend and Serenity restful blend essential oils. As I opened them and put a few drops in my hand to rub this wellbeing support onto the bottoms of my feet, the aroma already went to work. I was absorbing the cellular support through my palms and that natural chemistry was making its way to all parts of my body through my reflex points on my hands and feet. I rubbed the remaining oils on the back of my neck right where my skull and neck connect. The occiput, a direct line to my limbic brain, balanced the central controller of my fight or flight response. I inhaled a few long, slow, deep breaths from the soothing aroma off my hands. My heart seemed to sigh with relief returning to its normal resting rate. My breathing was no longer labored or stressed. I was relaxed and enjoyed some satisfying breaths as I let my breathing become an automatic unnoticed response once again.

Three minutes—that's all it took! I was fine. And I was stunned! I had been utilizing these essential oils successfully in our home for months, but amazement still filled me. How did that work? How did it work so fast? And I used so little of it! Why is no one talking about this? I have to share this! I know so many people who suffer from stress and none of them need be scared about what's happening anymore. What a relief I can bring to my friends and family. Isn't it so natural that as we find support that really works we want to share it with those we love and care about?

I realized I had been stressing myself out in a job with a very toxic work environment. I know now why I attracted this experience. In my amazement after those three minutes, I realized that we should all know more about essential oils. At least the ones who were open to learning about natural solutions for supporting physical and emotional wellbeing. I realized at that moment that I was changing my career to doTERRA and I would go wherever, whenever to educate and empower families to have access to this amazing affordable support. Two months later I quit that stressful job and haven't looked back.

It is my passion to empower those who want to learn more to know how to use the simple power of essential oils to take care of daily health needs (stress management, sleep quality, pain management, seasonal threats and discomfort.) If you are called to lead this movement like I was, I am equipped to mentor you to learn how to use these products, and how to keep this simple while we progressively build your financial future for your family legacy. We share these natural gifts as integrated medicine to save families time and money on healthcare. My customer group is growing into the multiple thousands all around the world.

I can show you how your own uniqueness is all that is required to be successful. I love to do this business while I enjoy my life working from home or traveling where and when I wish. It gives me freedom. Feel free to ask questions or seek more information by emailing me at nstrange@transformAnation.com. I am here to help you in any way I can.

Transform-A-Nation Sharing This Message

We have the power to transform this world. Communication is necessary to really connect. Conversations are key to develop new ideas. Leaders learn the most by listening to hear what is not being said but what is needed. Understanding is where our attention needs to focus so we don't develop resistance that stalls our progress. As we seek to know better our own selves, we can join in collaborative groups forming productive communities to reach out and thrive. It is possible to be your own unique self and to inspire others to discover their gifts and strengths. As we strive for higher emotional intelligence, we lead with a positive servant leadership style. This is how we transform-a-nation. It starts with you and I. It begins with our cells, minds and our bodies.

Book an interview, schedule an inspirational consultation to guide your development, or invite me to speak with your team, group or organization. Live speaking, video and phone conferencing available.

Ask for a free wellbeing consultation, or essential oil class, or for a sample of doTERRA essential oils and nutritional products, or seek information and a free demonstration of the 20-year proven circulation enhancement medical device that's so popular in thousands of hospitals around the world. The root cause of many symptoms can be traced back to poor nutrition, lack of cellular vitality, circulation issues and lack of proper hydration.

I enjoy inspiring everyone to learn to listen to what their body is saying through the symptoms and communications we can observe from the body's main wellness systems. Improved health becomes a result of returning to homeostasis—your body's natural, normal balance.

Norma Strange
(270) 634-5076
(629) 777-6540
nstrange@transformAnation.com
www.transformAnation.com

Learn more about our LIFE support community and collaborations. Message for mentoring, leadership, consultations, or speaking at your events.

How I Overflow... Leading 21st Century Wellbeing

For Families & Corporate Wellness Program Leaders: For me, getting to overflow into people's lives means connecting them, you, with a kind of health that is impactful from the inside out—Physically. I am passionate about leading the integrated medicine movement to educate and empower families to take control of their healthcare. I speak and educate people all over the world about three critical LIFE focus areas included in my 21rst Century Wellbeing concept: Cellular Wellness, Enhanced Circulation, and Hydration. As we educate families and inform corporate workplaces to educate on improving physical and emotional wellbeing, we will build stronger relationships and strengthen our communities as a result of more people taking personal responsibility for their LIFE to Let It Flow Effortlessly.

For Healthcare Professionals & Specialized Health Practitioners: In addition, we have a solution to offer better marketing touch points to engage, vitalize and grow customer reach for health professionals who offer services in their local communities. Imagine an effective, engaging marketing outreach that gets your customers coming in more frequently, adding new self-serve session revenue, and this new offering encourages them naturally to bring in their family members and other referrals. It's marketing that is so effective, it pays for itself over and over again! This is our health professional business program of LIFE – Let It (Cash)Flow Effortlessly and is offered to qualified businesses to support these businesses' operations and lessen the negative impact from increased health insurance costs and the difficulty in getting paid through insurance companies in a timely manner. We must support our local practitioners to survive and thrive in business so they are available to care for our communities.

----

www.NaturalSolutionsFirst.com

Improve your cellular health for improved physical and emotional wellbeing. Don't pay retail pricing—join with me as a wholesale customer or wellness advocate and save 25-55% on doTERRA essential oils, supplements and personal care products with a wholesale customer membership. Message for a free sample or details on our free membership offers.

----

www.yourwellness360.com/normastrange

Circulation enhancement for increased energy, mood improvement and better sleep quality from 8 minute session two times daily delivered from patented medical device. Message for more information and to arrange a free demonstration of this in-home healthcare medical device. For details on the device, becoming a distributor and for purchasing, visit www.norma-strange.bemergroup.com

ACKNOWLEDGEMENTS

I am so very thankful to God. I enjoy the process of becoming the best I can be and bringing out the best in others. My prayer is that I realize the potential God gave me, and that I may create impact sharing His love every day through whatever it is I do. I love the active command God inspired on my life to share HOPE – Helping Other People Everywhere, every day and in every way.

There are absolutely no words powerful enough to thank my husband, Greg, and my two daughters for the love, sacrifices and understanding they have given me. They understand how to share me with the world and they see me light up as I am utilized sharing my gifts and talents. I do love to see their eyes as I share the many miracles I see in may daily work. I am so grateful to have the honor to be in your lives!

And, to my mom who modeled strength and optimism for me as she raised me into the woman I am, thank you! I enjoy your friendship and support.

To my extended family, countless friends, mentors, advisors and coaches who've helped shape me to become the powerful leader I am, thank you. I appreciate all of the patience and love you've deposited in me along this journey. I hope to make you proud to be associated with me.

This project was brought to a level I could have only hoped for by a talented young visionary, Naomi Neal. She understood what I was trying to do with this work and she made it effortless to refine and arrange this conversation to come alive. I know now why we met through what seemed a random social media connection. Angels are noticed and sent our way to help when we are doing our greatest work. Thank you Naomi. This work wouldn't feel as alive without your help.

To the Morgan James Publishing team: Special thanks to David Hancock, CEO & Founder for believing in me and my message. To my Author Relations Manager, Bonnie Rauch, thanks for making the process seamless and easy. Many more thanks to everyone else, but especially Jim Howard, Bethany Marshall, and Nickcole Watkins.

ABOUT THE AUTHOR

Norma S. Strange is an international encouraging voice leading people to claim their power. Her mentoring, speaking and consulting elevates you to embrace your own uniqueness. She loves to mentor leaders and consult with business owners to inspire action as they believe their worth, own their identity, become effective and create more impact.

Her quick wit and vast entrepreneurial experience make her a valuable resource for creating breakthrough change in people who are ready to take the next step. She inspires action to foster quality relationships creating value in building better communities through genuine connection and collaboration.

She is a doTERRA essential oils distributor leading a large international team. She attracts and empowers families worldwide to learn and use essential oils for health independence and financial freedom. She knows integrated medicine will play a leading role in healthcare transformation saving families time and money while improving health.

It has always been her passion to assist businesses to market more effectively and create thriving success. She's added distributing a circulation enhancement device to assist health professionals to attract, retain and serve their current clients more effectively. Adding this device brings new clients, referrals, and creates an additional service revenue to these businesses. This program supports the business to stay profitable and capable to serve their community. Her program guides these health professionals to position their services to be at the center of their community building a robust referral and retention program. She believes helping these business owners win is important to keeping our communities educated and healthy.

She's been happily married for nearly thirty years to the man who made her "Strange." These two artists enjoy celebrating their daughters' own unique expressions as they gain their own footing and voice in this world. Casey has a wonderful inquisitive spirit and loves art, psychology, cares for the planet's sustainability, and has insatiable need to understand science and how things really work. Jessica possesses intuition to know just when to offer a hug to share unconditional love, loves art, photography, makeup, food and making homes and spaces around the world more beautiful.

WORKS CITED

A Bug's Life. Directed by John Lasseter. Performances by Kevin Spacey, Dave Foley, and Julia Louis-Dreyfus. Pixar Animation Studios, Walt Disney Pictures, 1998.

"Alexander Graham Bell Quotes." AZQuotes.com. Accessed 14 March 2018.

Atkinson, William Walker, *Thought Vibration Or, the Law of Attraction in the Thought World.* The New Thought Publishing Company, 1908.

Carnegie, Dale. *How to Win Friends and Influence People,* 1936.

"Charles Darwin Quotes." AZQuotes.com. Accessed 14 March 2018.

Covey, Stephen R. *The 7 Habits of Highly Effective People.* Free Press, 1989.

Gerber, Michael E. *The E-myth Revisited: Why Most Small Businesses Don't Work and What to Do About It.* HarperCollins, 1995.

"Helen Keller Quotes." AZQuotes.com. Accessed 14 March 2018.

"Henry Ford Quotes." BrainyQuote.com. Accessed March 10, 2018.

Hill, Napoleon. *Think and Grow Rich.* The Ralston Society, 1937.

InnSaei: The Power of Intuition. Directed by Hrund Gunnsteinsdottir and Kristín Ólafsdóttir. Zeitgeist Films, 2016.

It's a Wonderful Life. Directed by Frank Capra. Performances by Jimmy Stewart, Donna Reed, and Lionel Barrymore. RKO Radio Pictures, 1946.

"John Dewey Quotes." AZQuotes.com. Accessed 14 March 2018.

Jones, Charlie "Tremendous." *Quotes are Tremendous.* Tremendous Life Books, 1995.

Larsen, Gary. *The Far Side.* Universal Press Syndicate, 1980.

Lechter, Sharon and Greg S. Reid. *Three Feet From Gold: Turn Your Obstacles into Opportunities!* Sterling Publishing, 2009.

"Maxwell Maltz Quotes." AZQuotes.com. Accessed 14 March 2018.

Needham, Robert A. *Collaborative Commonwealth.* Robert A. Needham, 2014.

New American Standard Bible® (NASB). The Lockman Foundation, 1995. Used by permission.

Pay It Forward. Directed by Mimi Leder. By Catherine Ryan Hyde and Leslie Dixon. Performances by Kevin Spacey, Haley Joel Osment, and Helen Hunt. Warner Bros, 2000.

Secret. The. Directed by Rhonda Byrne. Prime Time Productions, 2007.

Sully. Directed by Clint Eastwood. Performances by Tom Hanks, Aaron Eckhart, and Laura Linney. Warner Brothers, 2016.

"Warren Buffett Quotes." AZQuotes.com. Accessed 14 March 2018.

Warren, Rick. *The Purpose Driven Life. Zondervan,* 2002.

"Wayne Dyer Quotes." AZQuotes.com. Accessed 14 March 2018.

Wilkinson, Bruce. *The Dream Giver.* Penguin Random House, 2003.

Williamson, Marianne. *Return to Love: Reflections on the Principles of a Course in Miracles.* HarperCollins, 1992. Quoted in *Akeelah and the Bee.* Directed by Doug Atchison. Performances by Angela Bassett, Laurence Fishburne, and Keke Palmer. Lionsgate Films and 2929, 2006.

"Zig Ziglar Quotes." AZQuotes.com. Accessed 14 March 2018.

Morgan James
Speakers Group

↗ www.TheMorganJamesSpeakersGroup.com

We connect Morgan James published
authors with live and online events
and audiences who will benefit
from their expertise.